D1554850

REIGNING WITH CHRIST

Lance Lambert

First Printing
1978

Second Printing
June, 1992

Available from:

Christian Tape Ministry
4424 Huguenot Road
Richmond, Virginia 23235

PRINTED IN U.S.A.

PREFACE

The following twelve messages were given by Lance Lambert, during 1976, at Halford House in Richmond, England. His spoken words have been transcribed into this book and edited only for clarity. These messages are printed by permission.

"And know I vest in you the kingship which my Father vested in me."

Through these messages Lance Lambert clearly reminds us that the calling of God for man is that we should have dominion over all things that He has created. This is our divine vocation as man. We are not to be defeated but to overcome, not to be subdued but to subdue. This is man's eternal vocation. *We are called to reign with Christ.*

Ruling, reigning, governing, administering, controlling, guarding, keeping or supervising are all facets of one single matter that God had in His mind in the very beginning when He created man in His image and after His likeness. God's purpose from the very beginning was that in union with Himself, man should come to the place of ruling and reigning, where he could administer the government of God.

The question is: Are we allowing the Holy Spirit to do that work in us today of forming the life of Christ in us, being conformed to His very character? Are we letting our self-life die that we would know what it is to reign with Christ now and be trained in learning how to overcome, how to possess our possessions, how to subdue the enemy, and how to nullify his power?

God has a plan for all of eternity and He calls us to reign with Him and administer His government. What the Lord's people must see is that in order to reign with God for eternity we must be trained today. God is not going to place people in responsibility if they are not trained, if the life of Christ is not formed in them. *We must learn to reign with Christ now.*

Do we desire that God's heart be satisfied, that His purpose be fulfilled? If we do then there is only one answer—die to self that we might reign with Christ. The original purpose for man was thwarted by sin, but thank God this matter of dominion over all things has been secured in the Lord Jesus Christ.

For the Lord's people today the critical issue is whether we are willing to go the whole way with God, to suffer, that we would reign with Christ today, overcoming the world in His life. If we do the reward is great.

We commit this book to the Lord and ask that He use it for His glory.

Christian Tape Ministry

CONTENTS

THE DIVINE PURPOSE FOR MAN

Dominion

Psalm 8—O Lord, our Lord, How excellent is Thy name in all the earth, Who hast set Thy glory upon the heavens! Out of the mouth of babes and sucklings hast thou established strength, Because of Thine adversaries, That Thou mightest still the enemy and the avenger. When I consider thy heavens, the work of thy fingers, The moon and the stars, which thou hast ordained; What is man, that thou art mindful of him? And the son of man, that thou visitest him? For thou hast made him but little lower than God, And crownest him with glory and honor. Thou makest him to have dominion over the works of thy hands; Thou hast put all things under his feet: All sheep and oxen, Yea, and the beasts of the field, The birds of the heavens, and the fish of the sea, Whatsoever passeth through the paths of the seas. O Lord, our Lord, How excellent is thy name in all the earth!

Luke 22:28-30—But ye are they that have continued with me in my temptations; And I appoint unto you a kingdom, even as my Father appointed unto me, that ye may eat and drink at my table in my kingdom; and ye shall sit on thrones judging the twelve tribes of Israel.

Luke 22:29—I vest in you the kingship which my Father vested in me. (New English Bible)

By the grace of God and by the enabling of the Holy Spirit, we want to look at this whole subject of our eternal vocation. There is no subject that has more real and concrete effect upon our lives than this matter: foreordained to rule, called to the throne, or called to reign. It is not that we might become more vague and abstract and lost in another world. It is that we might see the very real relationship that reigning with Christ has with our life down here, first in our relationship to one another in Christ, then our relationship in homes and families, our relationship in business and work, and our relationship to the world.

To the men who had lived with Him for three years and knew Him closely and intimately, all of whom were to fall away, all of whom were to deny Him (some more terribly than the others), all of whom were to come through shaved of their self-manufactured Christianity and self-produced service to a new place in Christ, Jesus said, *"I vest in you the kingship which My Father vested in me."*

Then in Psalm 8, what is the connection between the Lord's name being excellent in all the earth, and babes and sucklings being used to still the enemy and the avenger? To the superficial reader, this must seem to be a jumble of ideas. But, that is exactly what this Psalm is all about. It is about reigning. The most comforting thing about this Psalm is not that God speaks of the mighty, the strong, the great, or the knowledgeable, but He speaks of babes and sucklings. The Spirit of God can take hold of them and do such a work in their lives that the enemy and the avenger is stilled. That is a wonderful thing!

The rest of Psalm 8 continues with the purpose of God for man. It is a very good thing for us as believers to ask ourselves: What was God's real purpose for man in the beginning? Why did He create man? Why was man created in a way that none of the rest of the natural creation was created? What was God's purpose in creating man in His image and after His likeness? It is very simply that he should have **dominion.** In union with God, he should rule and govern the whole universe. He should reign over the earth and the heavens. He should administer the government of God and administer the will of God. He should control the earth; he should control the world. He should guard it, keep it, and supervise it.

You can use all these words: *rule, reign, govern, administer, control, guard, keep, or supervise.* They are all little facets of one single matter that God had in His mind in the very beginning when He created man in His image and after His likeness. It was not that man should just be a little creature that stood in awe of Him all his days. It was not that he should be someone who was instructed, but never came to a place of supervision where he could supervise or administer. God's purpose in man from the very beginning was that in union with Himself, he should come to the place of ruling and reigning, where he could administer the government of God. This is very important.

Such dominion, according to the Scripture, is not just a matter of mere title or position or status. Often people think that if a person has a position, he is naturally qualified. In our bureaucracy today, we find that many people who have positions are not really capable of the position they hold. They have a title, but they are really incapable of exercising the authority that goes with that title. They are unable to discharge the responsibility that goes with their status or with their position.

We seem to think that God creates automatons, automatic machines. Somehow or other He can just say, "You are a king," and then you are a king. But that is not so. The one thing the Bible reveals from Genesis to Revelation is that kingship is not a matter of title or status or position. We find in the Word of God men who had the status, the title, the position, and the pedigree who were anything but royal in character.

Our Lord Jesus came with a pedigree that was absolutely genuine and above question, with a title that was divinely given, with a status that none of us can have. Nevertheless, He was made perfect through sufferings and He learned obedience by the things which He suffered. In other words, He came to a place of completeness. He was trained even as the Son, the Son of Man, to the place of responsibility. The Lord Jesus displayed and exhibited a kind of royalty this world knows nothing about even when He was stripped of every single thing that goes with the mystique of royalty. When He was stripped naked and beaten black and blue, when His beard was pulled out, when He was bloodied, bruised and lacerated, still He revealed an inner kingliness. He revealed an inner royalty of character. *That* kind of person can do no other than reign. You can strip them of everything, but in the end they *have* to reign. They can do no other.

Even if God wanted to give you a title and a position, this question of dominion is not just a matter of a title. You have to come to the place where you can exercise the authority and discharge the responsibility that goes with that position. In other words, having dominion, as the Scripture speaks of it, requires not only union with God, but the development of spiritual character. It needs training.

When we turn to the very beginning, in the very first recorded words that God spoke to man, we read:

> *And God said, Let us make man in our image, after our likeness: and let them have dominion over the fish of the sea, and over the birds of the heavens, and over the cattle, and over all the earth, and over every creeping thing that creepeth upon the earth. And God blessed them: and God said unto them, Be fruitful, and multiply, and replenish the earth, and subdue it; and have dominion over the fish of the sea, and over the birds of the heavens, and over every living thing that moveth upon the earth. (Genesis 1:26, 28)*

In the Authorized Version, the Revised Version, the American Standard Version, and the Revised Standard Version, the word *dominion* is translated, "and let him have dominion." In the New American Standard Bible they have translated it, "and let him rule," which is a much simpler way of putting it. We have this same Hebrew word in Psalm 49:

> *They are appointed as a flock for Sheol; Death shall be their shepherd: And the upright shall have dominion over them in the morning; and their beauty shall be for Sheol to consume, that there be no habitation for it. (Psalm 49:14)*

> *The Lord will send forth the rod of thy strength out of Zion: Rule thou in the midst of thine enemies. (Psalm 110:2)*

The word *rule* there is the same word, "have dominion." It is very interesting that of the second Man, the last Adam, it is said, "Have dominion over thine enemies...rule thou in the midst of thine enemies." This Hebrew word means simply: "to have dominion, to rule, or to dominate." The most common English translation of the word *dominion* according to the Oxford Dictionary is: "the power and right of governing and controlling." *And let them have the power and right of governing and controlling.*

A second definition is: "sovereign authority, rule or control." The very first words that God ever uttered to man that are recorded in the Word were to *have dominion, rule, have the right and power to govern and control.* This is at the very beginning of the human story. And God said unto them, "Be fruitful, and multiply, and replenish the earth, and subdue it" (Genesis 1:28). Please note those two words *replenish* and *subdue.* It does not say replenish and subdue the garden, but it says replenish the earth, and subdue it.

Compare that with Genesis 2:15: "And the Lord God took the man, and put him into the garden of Eden to dress it and to keep it." Again we have a very interesting thought here because this word *keep:* (to dress, or till, or cultivate, as you have in some of the modern versions) comes from the same root as the word *to watch, to guard, to keep, to observe, to care.* Man was told to have dominion over the whole earth; but first, God put him into a garden that He Himself had planted and ordered out of chaos and confusion. God placed man in that garden and told him to cultivate it, till it, dress it and keep it, guard it, watch it. Then, as man came into a union with God, he was to move out from that garden and subdue the whole earth. He was to begin with the garden and then to go out.

Why did he need to subdue the earth? Most Christians have got the idea that when God created everything, every single thing was perfect. In one sense, if you want to say that there was no disorder, there is probably much truth in that. However, life is life and life has to be trained.

It is so interesting that God said, "subdue it." Why does it need to be subdued? People seem to think that without any sin there was no need for subduing anything; everything just grew into perfect place. You went out and the flowers were there and there were no weeds. Later, God cursed the ground and said, "Thorns and thistles shall it bear." However, the point is that there was a need to have dominion. Even when man had not sinned, before he fell, there was a need in a world in which there was no sin for man to have dominion. If man did not have dominion, things would start to get out of hand. He had to cultivate it. There would have to be a pruning; there would have to be a cutting back; there would have to be a training.

Man was in the garden to learn his first simple lessons in a very happy surrounding. God walked in this garden every day and there was the tree of life in the center and the tree of the knowledge of good and evil somewhere else in that garden. It was not as if God just said, "Have dominion," and man had dominion. The point was that God was training man, first in the garden, in a certain limited area with a boundary, then from that to the whole earth. And then what? Do you think that God's training of man was to end just with a physical subduing, training and cultivating of the earth? Doesn't it seem to you that having taught first the natural, then He would have gone on to the spiritual, and that man, in union with God, would have known what it was to control the universe? After all, even fallen man can get a man to the moon and back. It is not as if God did not put this genius into man. It was all put there by God. It is because we have been made in the likeness of God and after His image that we have this genius, but it is corrupted; it is fallen. It is a very interesting thing, by the way, concerning "dress and keep it" that it is exactly the same Hebrew word that you have in Genesis 3:24:

> So he drove out the man; and he placed at the east of the garden of Eden the Cherubim, and the flame of a sword which turned every way, to keep the way of the tree of life.

There are many terms in the Bible by which God takes up this matter of having dominion, of ruling, or reigning or administering the government of God, the will of God on the earth. Jesus put it in a very simple way when He taught us to pray in the pattern prayer, "Thy kingdom come, Thy will be done, as it is in heaven, so on earth." It is not, "Oh Lord, may Your will come to pass one day, somehow or other after you return."

We are meant to declare that the will of God in our own circumstances should be fulfilled, in the circumstances of the church in which we are found, and in the circumstances of the community, even though it is unsaved and lying in the evil one.

We are custodians of the will and government of God. Therefore, as those who have not only been created by God, but redeemed by God, we are meant to be the ones who administer the will of God.

God speaks in a number of terms in connection with this matter. Let us consider a few of them.

Throne

He raiseth up the poor out of the dust, He lifteth up the needy from the dunghill, To make them sit with princes, And inherit the throne of glory: For the pillars of the earth are the Lord's, And he hath set the world upon them. (I Samuel 2:8)

This is the song of Hannah about Samuel, who never became king. What a remarkable statement for Hannah to make! There, by the Spirit of God, Hannah saw something that was the very heart of the purpose of God: to take men and women like you and me who have fallen so deeply and so terribly into sin and darkness and bondage, and cause us, by His grace, to "inherit the throne of glory." How wonderful then when you listen to these words:

And the God of all grace, who called you unto his eternal glory in Christ, after that ye have suffered a little while, shall himself perfect, establish, strengthen you. (I Peter 5:10)

Thy throne, O God, is for ever and ever: A scepter of equity is the scepter of thy kingdom. (Psalm 45:6)

Whatever happens down here on this level, in this dimension, the fact remains that God's throne is for ever and ever.

A glorious throne, set on high from the beginning, is the place of our sanctuary. (Jeremiah 17:12)

That is a most remarkable statement for a man to make who has seen not only the city of God and the temple of God destroyed, but the people dispersed. Even if he said it before it happened, he knew it was going to happen because he had said it again and again. The whole people were under the hand of God in judgment. They were going to be sent away into captivity for seventy years and at least a fifty year exile. Yet he says, "A glorious throne, set on high from the beginning, is the place of our sanctuary." If only believers, under the new covenant, had seen that. From the very beginning, the church is the place for the authority of God. If we had seen that it was the place for the exercise of the authority of God, the place in which and through which Christ was to rule in the midst of His enemies, we would begin to understand the need of being trained. We would begin to understand the need to discharge our responsibilities as believers as far as the kingdom of God goes.

The throne does not mean just a beautiful ornate throne with someone sitting there with wonderful regalia. God is not the least bit interested in that; it is all secondary. No one will ever have worn what the Lord Jesus will wear. They will never be vested with the regalia He will have; nevertheless, that is still all very secondary. The thing about the throne of God is that it stands for sovereign authority and for divine government.

It is just that point of divine government and sovereign authority that has been challenged by the powers of darkness. "I will be like the Most High," is what Lucifer, the day star, said. "I will exalt my throne above the stars of God." "I...I...I..." It was a challenge to divine government, a challenge to the sovereign authority of God and of His Christ by what the Bible calls "the anointed cherub that covereth."

This world is essentially a spiritual world. We think of us as having a physical life now and one day we are going to have a kind of spiritual life; but in actual fact, this whole world is essentially a spiritual world. The things which are seen only represent things which are not seen, and all the things which are not seen are in one way or another influencing the things which are visible. All of human history, the history of the nations, the history of the Gentiles, and the history of Israel is summed up by this tremendous challenge to divine government and sovereign authority on the part of the devil. From the very beginning of the record in the Bible, the powers of darkness and the power of light have been engaged in battle. That is why you find wonderful words such as these:

> *Why do the nations rage,*
> *And the peoples meditate a vain thing?*
> *The kings of the earth set themselves,*
> *And the rulers take counsel together,*
> *Against the Lord, and against his anointed, saying,*
> *Let us break their bonds asunder,*
> *And cast away their cords from us.*
> *He that sitteth in the heaven will laugh:*
> *The Lord will have them in derision.*
> *Then will he speak unto them in his wrath,*
> *And vex them in his sore displeasure:*
> *Yet I have set my king upon my holy hill of Zion.*
> *(Psalm 2:1-6)*

> *The Lord saith unto my Lord,*
> *Sit thou at my right hand,*
> *Until I make thine enemies thy footstool.*
> *The Lord will send forth the rod of thy strength*
> *   out of Zion:*
> *Rule thou in the midst of thine enemies.*
> *Thy people offer themselves willingly*
> *In the day of thy power, in holy array.*
> *(Psalm 110:1-3)*

You will find this matter of the throne all the way through the Bible, from the beginning right the way through. Although it is not revealed in the first few books of the Bible, yet increasingly, as you go on into the Bible you are taken back to the beginning and before times eternal. You see that there was a throne set and upon that throne One whom the Father determined to be the anointed One, the Christ. Then you find that there is a power of darkness, this being we call Satan, the devil, who challenged that determination of God to give that place to the Son. From then on, we have the whole of human history, right the way through to the very end of the Bible where we read these wonderful words in Revelation 22:

> *And the throne of God and of the Lamb are therein and His servants shall serve Him . . . and they shall reign for ever and ever. (verse 3b, 5b)*

That is the last word, more or less, of the Bible. Does that give you some understanding of what Jesus meant in Revelation 3:21? In the last word to the seventh church that He had been speaking to as representing the whole church in time and in locality on earth, He says:

> *He that overcometh, I will give to him to sit down with me in my throne, as I also overcame, and sat down with my Father in his throne.*

Reign

> *And there shall be no curse any more: and the throne of God and of the Lamb shall be therein: and his servants shall serve him; and they shall see his face; and his name shall be on their foreheads. And there shall be night no more; and they need no light of lamp, neither light of sun; for the Lord God shall give them light: and they shall reign for ever and ever. (Revelation 22:3-5)*

> *If we endure, we shall also reign with him: if we shall deny him, he also will deny us. (II Timothy 2:12)*

Please note carefully that there is an "if" here. "If we endure..." In your old version it is "suffer." It is the same thought. You do not just suffer, you endure. You go right through. You do not just sit down and make a meal of it, but while you are suffering, you endure because you are coming right through, you are going on. "If we endure, we shall also reign with Him."

Kings

> *He made us to be kings and priests unto his God and Father; to him be the glory and the dominion for ever and ever. (Revelation 1:6)*

In some of the modern versions it says, "He made them to be a kingdom, priests unto His God and Father."

Worthy art thou to take the book, and to open the seals thereof: for thou wast slain, and didst purchase unto God with thy blood men of every tribe, and tongue, and people, and nation, and madest them to be unto our God a kingdom and priests; and they reign upon the earth. (Revelation 5:9-10)

Notice that it does not say, "They *shall* reign upon the earth." It says, "They reign upon the earth and they have been made kings and priests." Again, some of the modern versions say, "Have been made a kingdom and priests unto God." The Revised Standard Version and the New American Standard Bible all render it kingdom. "He has made us a kingdom, priests unto His God and Father." It is because some of the most authentic manuscripts have the word *kingdom* instead of *kings* in them. It is based on Exodus 19:6: "And ye shall be unto me a kingdom of priests, and a holy nation."

This word *kingdom* is one of the most difficult Greek words to translate accurately in English. It is an abstract noun denoting sovereignty or royal power or dominion. That is why dear Mr. Sparks always used to render it by *kingship*. However, you cannot say He has made us "kingship." It is only later that it became a concrete noun meaning territory and people ruled over. But all of us, as soon as we think of the word kingdom, think of the people and territory ruled over; we do not think of the throne.

When you think of the United Kingdom, you think of the territory of the British Isles and the people, the nation. When you think of the Kingdom of Nepal, you think of the territory of Nepal, the nation and the people which are ruled over. But in the Greek it has much more of the idea first of the sovereignty, the royal power, the dominion. When you understand that, it makes you realize we have been called to something. God has made us not only a kingdom, but He has made us a sovereign power. He has made us a royal power. He has given us a dominion. We have to exercise something and that is why it says, "And they reign upon the earth." Priests do not reign, and the kingdom (in one sense) does not reign; the king reigns. You have got this wonderful crossbreeding of an idea, and when you begin to see it like that, it becomes more and more wonderful.

> *And raised us up with him, and made us to sit with him in the heavenly places in Christ Jesus. (Ephesians 2:6)*

This is a wonderful word given to every believer. We have not only been made alive together with Christ, raised up together with Christ, but we have been made to sit together with Christ. Where is Christ sitting? He is sitting at the right hand of God the Father. Where are you and I? We have been made to sit together with Him in heavenly places. That is a tremendous thing.

> *Which he wrought in Christ, when he raised him from the dead, and made him to sit at his right hand in the heavenly places, far above all rule, and authority, and power, and dominion, and every name that is named, not only in this world, but also in that which is to come: and he put all things in subjection under his feet, and gave him to be head over all things to the church, which is his body, the fulness of him that filleth all in all. (Ephesians 1:20-23)*

> *And you did he make alive, when ye were dead through your trespasses and sins. (Ephesians 2:1)*

If we could only see this, what a difference it would make to our church gatherings, to our fellowship, to our relationship to the Lord, to our relationship to one another. Suddenly everything would begin to fall into place. God has not just brought us together to be a kind of social club, nor even just to help each other, nor only to build one another up. Even our building of one another up has an aim: that we might take the position that God wants us to take in the unseen, in the heavenly places and rule. Church history would have been so different if we had seen it in that light.

And there was given him dominion, and glory, and a kingdom, that all the peoples, nations, and languages should serve him: his dominion is an everlasting dominion, which shall not pass away, and his kingdom that which shall not be destroyed. (Daniel 7:14)

But the saints of the Most High shall receive the kingdom, and possess the kingdom for ever, even for ever and ever. (verse 18)

What is the difference between receiving a kingdom and possessing a kingdom? Daniel wants to make it abundantly clear that this is not anything transient; it is not just a millennial reign. This is for ever and ever.

Until the ancient of days came, and judgment was given to the saints of the Most High, and the time came that the saints possessed the kingdom. And the kingdom and the dominion, and the greatness of the kingdoms under the whole heaven, shall be given to the people of the saints of the Most High: his kingdom is an everlasting kingdom, and all dominions shall serve and obey him. Here is the end of the matter. (verse 22, 27-28)

Jesus said, "I have appointed unto you a kingdom." The New English Bible puts it, "I vest in you the kingship which my Father vested in me." How beautifully put! It is just so delicately translated that it gets at the whole heart of the matter.

Head and Body

And he is the head of the body, the church: who is the beginning, the firstborn from the dead; that in all things he might have the preeminence. (Colossians 1:18)

And he put all things in subjection under his feet, and gave him to be head over all things to the church, which is his body, the fulness of him that filleth all in all. (Ephesians 1:22-23)

What does it mean? Surely it means that if we are a body joined to a Head and therefore the living, functioning counterpart of the Head, the complement of the Head, the expression of the Head, it must have something to do with the will of the Head. There must be something the Head wants to do in Britain, that the Head wants to do in the world. He wants to do things. It is not good enough for us to say, "Oh, isn't it wonderful, we are one with Him." What does the Head want to do? How does He want to express His mind? How does He want to express His will? How does He want to fulfill His ministry? The Head has a ministry toward this world to be discharged. We have a responsibility to see that the mind of the Head is known, obeyed, and the responsibility discharged.

City

> *And I saw the holy city, new Jerusalem, coming down out of heaven from God, made ready as a bride adorned for her husband...And there came one of the seven angels who had the seven bowls, who were laden with the seven last plagues; and he spake with me, saying, Come hither, I will show thee the bride, the wife of the Lamb. And he carried me away in the Spirit to a mountain great and high, and showed me the holy city Jerusalem, coming down out of heaven from God, having the glory of God. (Revelation 21:2,9,10,11a)*

I have said many times that the Bible ends with a city. Yet, it seems to me that if we say the Bible ends with a city, many people might miss the whole point. They might get hold of the fact that in the end the objective of God is a bride for His Son, but miss the point that the bride, the wife of the Lamb, is a city. A man does not usually refer to his wife as a city. London has never been called a bride. What is this strange cross-pollination of ideas? What does it mean, "The wife of the Lamb" is "the city?"

A city is essentially a center of government. It is where an administration is centered. Generally speaking, it extends over quite an area. What do you think a city really symbolizes, as opposed to a household, or a family, or the temple, or the body? It surely must mean it is a center of administration, a center of government. A city would be a helpless jumble if there were not some kind of administration of government, if there were not some kind of order observed. That is really the heart of this whole matter.

One side of the coin is intimacy or union. God loves us so much that He looks upon us as His bride, as the one He wants to share His life with, that He wants to share Himself with, that He wants to be joined to. He wants to live out the whole of eternity with us. That is one glorious side of it. Of course, it is much more than that because we know that Eve was taken out of Adam and formed "bone of his bone and flesh of his flesh." We know that the second Man, the last Adam, was put to sleep and His side was pierced. John makes very much of that side being opened and blood and water coming out. Later in his letter he says that there are three that bear witness, the Spirit, the blood and the water. He was tremendously strong. It has nothing to do with the finished work of Christ because Jesus had already said, "finished." Why was John so amazingly arrested by the piercing of His side and the water and blood that came out? It was the second Man, the last Adam, and through that blood and water that came out of His side the church has been formed. It was a most wonderful picture. The apostle speaks of it in Ephesians 5: "This mystery is great, but I speak of Christ and the church."

The other side of the coin is that this bride has been trained to rule. She is not just being a sweet, loving bride who makes a lovely home and a place of rest for her husband and becomes, as it were, a means of his comfort and encouragement. It is that there is a place of government. This bride has been trained to reign, trained to administer divine government, and trained for all eternity, whatever God is going to do in eternity. Never think for a single moment that this is all that God has ever thought up. Some people seem to think this world is literally the sum of God's genius. We know men have been to the moon and they have told us that it is gray like some kind of deserted, volcanic wilderness. But you must never think that when God has got rid of all the sin that He is not going to do something new. When that whole parenthesis of sin and sorrow and mourning and death has passed away, He says, "Old things have passed away, behold I make all things new." There will be new heavens and new earths, new universes, new suns. I am quite sure God has got all kind of things (if I may say it reverently) up His sleeve, but He will not do it without us. We are to be the people. It is as if He says, "I cannot do it. I will not do it. I must have the people who can administer the government. I must have the people who can control. I must have the people who can supervise, who can have the dominion."

> *But ye are come unto mount Zion, and unto the city of the living God, the heavenly Jerusalem. (Hebrews 12:22)*

> *For we have not here an abiding city, but we seek after the city which is to come. (Hebrews 13:14)*

In one place he says, "Ye are come..." And in the other place he says, "We seek after the city." That is the whole paradox of this matter of learning how to reign. In one sense, spiritually, we have arrived; in the other sense, spiritually, we are on a pilgrimage. On one side we have been given authority in the name of Christ. It is as if God said, "If you don't, I won't." I noted down something that dear Mildred Cable said years ago: "Without God we cannot; without us God will not." It is so true. It is not as if God cannot. Of course He can! He can do without us. We are just a load of trouble, but the point is God will not. That is the marvelous thing. It is as if He loves us so much He says, "You have to learn. If you want to have a mess, have a mess. Don't expect Me always to carry you. You have to learn to exercise authority in the secret place. You have to learn to rule things for Me." You have to learn how to take that place in the unseen and determine the very course of your nation; not what *you* think it ought to be politically or anything else, but what is the will of God for that nation.

Why should we just throw in the glove and give everything over to the enemy before it is time? We know "the night comes when no man can work." Why should we make the night come one single minute before it is time? Isn't it enough for the night to come when no man can work? Why should the enemy push it on us ten years, twenty years before? And he will! The enemy is just like that. If he can extend anything like that, he will do it. And if we, as the people of God, are not alive, are not moving with Him and know covering and know how to be together in Him, our life hid with Christ in God, then we are unable to determine things. We are unable to hold things for God. It is to this that we who have been redeemed by God, are called. It is not merely to be a holy temple in the Lord, nor even the habitation of God in the spirit, nor even the body of Christ, as marvelous as that is. We are called to the throne to reign with Him.

THE ON-HIGH CALLING

I therefore, the prisoner in the Lord, beseech you to walk worthily of the calling wherewith ye were called. (Ephesians 4:1)

It is marvelous to be called to be the bride of Christ, called to be in union with Christ, but it is even more wonderful to think that we are called to the throne to reign with Him. I think that is simply incredible.

To the end that ye should walk worthily of God, who calleth you into his own kingdom and glory. (I Thessalonians 2:12)

I press on toward the goal unto the prize of the high calling of God in Christ Jesus. (Philippians 3:14)

This is one of the most remarkable chapters in the New Testament because in it the apostle Paul says that he counts everything but refuse. He does not even count that he himself has yet laid hold of that for which God has taken hold of him, but he presses on. What does he press on toward? "I press on to the goal unto the prize of the high calling of God in Christ Jesus." It is literally "the on-high calling." Isn't that amazing? The thought is the throne. It is that we are called not only to be part of the city, but we are called into divine government.

Which is a manifest token of the righteous judgment of God; to the end that ye may be counted worthy of the

kingdom of God, for which ye also suffer. (II
Thessalonians 1:5)

Why does it say, "...that ye may be counted worthy..."?
Surely it is all of grace. Here you have the other side. We do
not lose our place in the kingdom of God. If we have been
born of God, we have been born into the kingdom of heaven,
but we can lose our place in divine government. No one is
ever going to tell me that Christians who have got hearts as
narrow as a pea and an understanding of the Lord almost as
narrow, are one day going to sit on golden thrones judging this
world. It will be a total mess. It will only be if God can do
something in us through the things which we suffer, through
the training, through the discipline, through our relationship
one to another, through the inexplicable things that happen in
our circumstances and in our lives, that we can be brought to
the place where we learn the principles of divine government.

*For thus shall be richly supplied unto you the entrance
into the eternal kingdom of our Lord and Saviour
Jesus Christ.* (II Peter 1:11)

If we have been born of God, we are in the kingdom; we
don't lose our place; but, this is speaking of government. This
is speaking of the other side—sovereign power and sovereign
dominion. What a thing it is to be able to die like the apostle
Paul; to have run the race, finished the course, discharged the
ministry and know in your spirit that you can go into the presence of God, a richly supplied entrance into the government
of God. Oh, that is something!

I have always found the last words of C.T. Studd, when he
was dying, so very, very moving. When they asked him if he
had anything to say, he said these simple, but profound words:
"I can only say that of all God has ever asked me to do, I have
done everything." I think that is the most wonderful thing, to
be able to die and to be able to say that of all that God has
ever asked me to do, I have done. After all, that is all that
God requires of you. The mother of our Lord said to those
servants, "Whatsoever He saith, do it." In those simple words
of hers is the key to the Christian life, the key to Christian

growth, the key to Christian service and the key to church life. "Whatsoever He saith, do it."

> *The Lord will deliver me from every evil work, and will save me unto his heavenly kingdom. (II Timothy 4:18)*

The apostle Paul is a most disturbing man, isn't he? He is already saved, but he speaks here of being delivered from every evil work and preserved unto his heavenly kingdom. I believe he meant this: I do not want to lose my place in the divine government. That is why he said in one place, "I do not want to come to the place where I preach to others and I myself am a reject." He did not mean unsaved. He meant that having preached to others and helping others into the kingdom, into Christ, into salvation, then he finds that he himself is a reject as far as divine government goes, as far as inheritance goes. For the same apostle said that we can be saved so as by fire; we can lose everything, wood, hay, stubble, all burnt up.

> *Confirming the souls of the disciples, exhorting them to continue in the faith, and that through many tribulations we must enter into the kingdom of God. (Acts 14:22)*

> *For ye received not the spirit of bondage again unto fear; but ye received the spirit of adoption, whereby we cry, Abba, Father. The Spirit himself beareth witness with our spirit, that we are children of God: and if children, then heirs; heirs of God, and joint-heirs with Christ; if so be that we suffer with him, that we may be also glorified with him. (Romans 8:15-17)*

Now there is an "if." We do not lose our salvation, but it says, "if we suffer with him, we shall also be glorified with him." We shall know what it is to enter into the inheritance. Otherwise, we do not lose our salvation, but we lose our inheritance.

Thus we find these things which we can sum up. First, we have God's original purpose that man should have dominion with and in and by God. That was God's original purpose for man.

Secondly, we have the fall and enslavement of man. There is no distinction, "All have sinned and fallen short of the glory of God." There is a different kind of man now. We are different. Our constitution has changed from the way we were created. Still we bear in ourselves, constitutionally, some marks of being made in the image of God and after His likeness; but, a corruption and a perversion and a depraving has taken place. We are enslaved.

We are enslaved to material things. Think of the whole world around us. There is no understanding of their souls, no understanding of the spirit, no understanding of that invisible world. People spend their whole life building up their own little empire which, of necessity, they must leave when they die.

Then you have got enslavement to the physical. There are all kinds of things, whether it is career, or sex, or whatever else it is, we find an enslavement. We have it in Genesis 3. In itself there is nothing wrong, but something has come in.

Basically, man's constitution has changed from being what he was meant to be, a God-centered being, to a self-centered being. With that self-centeredness has come self-consciousness and self-sufficiency. Of course it is stupid. We were never made to be self-sufficient. People go around saying, "I am independent; I am going to be independent," gritting their teeth. It is a kind of obstinacy. We were never meant to be independent. It is not that we were meant to be dependent on one another, but we are meant to come into union with God and find our sufficiency in God. Then we become a true human being and only then. We are not real human beings until we find our union with God. In Scripture it speaks of people who are like brute beasts. They come to God and come into a union with God and then for the first time they begin to discover the meaning of life, the meaning of their own constitution and the meaning of salvation.

We are enslaved to spiritual powers, too. When you think of it, the people who are atheists are the most enslaved to spiritual powers that blind them and dilute them and deceive them. You find other people in things like spiritism and other cults where they are blinded and possessed and enslaved and fettered. They will not come near the gospel and they are unable to make a move toward the Lord Jesus.

Then we find Christ, the answer, God's answer, that second Man, the last Adam (see I Corinthians 15:45,47). He is a man in union with the Father and He does everything from the Father in Him. He says, "I do not speak of Myself, I speak as the Father speaks in Me." He only works the works He sees His Father doing. He says, "What is the will of My Father, that I do." Everything is from the Father in Him. Even as the Son, He still does everything from the Father in Him. He is teaching us a great lesson. "To him that overcometh will I grant to sit down with me in my throne even as I overcame." It is the Father in Him.

Another thing about Him is that He learned through the things He suffered. We find that in Hebrews 5:8,9. He was perfected through obedience. That does not mean there was anything wrong with him, but He came to full maturity by learning obedience through the things He suffered. He learned a discipline, He learned a training, and through that learning of obedience He learned first to come to full stature. If the Lord Jesus needed that, how much more do you and I need it. If before He could come to the throne He had to learn obedience through the things which He suffered, and being perfected go to the cross for us, and then beyond the cross to the throne, how much more should you and I.

We need to allow the Spirit of God to discipline us, to bring us to the place where we learn obedience through the things which we suffer. We do not like that. We prefer to grow like a little potted plant without anyone pinching any shoots out or cutting anything back or training us in any way. We just want to ramble where we want. "Oh," we say, "we are alive. That is the thing that matters, to be alive. The more alive we are the better it is." We have a shoot go out that way and a shoot go out that way and a shoot down that way. We do not want training. We want to go to some group where we are happy and where we can grow. We do not want anyone sitting on that shoot, and cutting back this and pinching out that and saying, "Now you have to go this way." We do not want that kind of thing, but that is what God has to do with us. The more we say, "No, no, no, I am going to be on my own; I know what the Lord wants for me," the less we learn and the more we disqualify ourselves from divine government. It is just in these little things that we learn the great lessons of divine government.

We see our Lord as the last Adam, the Second Man, reigning. It does not matter where we turn, we find Him reigning. When they had no food, He was in command of the situation. When Lazarus died, even when He wept, He was in command of the situation. When there was a storm and they all panicked, He was in command of the situation. He was in command. He was reigning all the time. Even when it says His soul was troubled, even when it says He became indignant, even when He made a whip of cords and drove them out of the temple, He was always in command; He was reigning. He learned to reign inwardly. He was denied an outward throne, denied any greater claim. Finally, they stripped Him of everything, and when they had stripped Him of everything, He reigned supreme. That is why some of the old church fathers always said that Psalm 98 was originally, "He reigneth from the tree." We do not know whether that really is true, but they say it was and the last words were cut out. Of course, people did not like the idea that it referred to the Messiah being crucified. But the fact of the matter is that it is the truth, He reigned from the tree.

Lastly, by becoming a sacrifice for us, He brings many sons to glory, and in Christ, God's original purpose for us is realized. That is why we have that wonderful word:

> *According to the eternal purpose which he purposed in Christ Jesus our Lord.* (Ephesians 3:11)

The Amplified Version puts it, "*...realized in Christ Jesus our Lord.*" Another version is, "*...showed forth in Christ Jesus our Lord.*" What does it mean? It means simply that in Christ, God has already won. He has realized His eternal purpose in Him and we, saved by Christ, in union with God in Him, anointed in Him, made one body in Him, are being trained for the throne. "If we suffer with Him that we may also be glorified with Him." Therefore, the purpose of God is not only to save us, not only to bring us to our own experience of His life, of His power, of His fulness, not only to build us together in Himself, but to train us to have dominion even in the humblest of circumstances.

It has not been given to all of us to have the afflictions of traveling all over the world, nor is it given to all of us to have the afflictions of having a platform ministry. Most of us have the afflictions of a kitchen sink or some dreadfully dull office where everyone appears to be mundane and dreary. But it is just there that the hand of God is training us. It is in these situations where it does not seem to matter, where at times it does not seem as if anyone would bother anyway, that this whole matter of being trained to have dominion is so important. It is the sphere of it.

The last word of the Bible is, *"They shall reign for ever and ever."* It is not even the bride or the city. Therefore, we must take note of the "ifs." There are enough "ifs" in these scriptures to give us sober thoughts. It is solemnizing: "If we endure with Him, we shall reign with Him. If we suffer with Him, we shall also be glorified with Him. Many contend, only one wins the race. To him that overcomes will I grant to sit down with Me in My throne."

Therefore we see three things in the Bible: Christ, the church, and the overcomer. When the majority of the saved do not go on, do not possess the will of God, do not fulfill the ministry God has given them, the Lord takes up a few, sometimes one, sometimes a remnant, who possess for the rest. It matters not what you call them: the overcomer, the remnant, or what else. They are the advance working party, and I think it is the loveliest way of describing them. They go ahead to get the whole thing done for the rest. They do not think, "We are something. We have gone on ahead of the whole blind, deluded, lethargic, worldly lot. We are, of course, an overcoming community. Belonging to us, you are of necessity, an overcomer. Because it really costs, we get the best. We know the Lord is really with us."

That is a kind of elitism. And that is what has been associated with the overcomer teaching and has destroyed it. It produced in some people a kind of superiority, "We are the overcomers. We are going to reign, by the grace of God of course, but we are going to reign because we are ready to suffer." That is a sure sign you are no overcomer; that is the very spirit that has wrecked everything all the way through. It was certainly not Mrs. Penn Lewis's idea, or D.M. Panton's idea, or Austin Sparks's idea, or Watchman Nee's idea, all of whom believed in this matter.

The fact of the matter is that these overcomers are harbingers. A harbinger is literally someone who goes ahead to find lodgings. He is a forerunner, a pioneer. Think of them as harbingers, an advance working party. They go on, not that they may be something and when the rest come they say, "Well, you made it." But they are there to welcome the rest. They are there because they have laid down their lives for the rest in order that the rest may come in. Now, for me, that transforms the whole matter of overcoming. However you look at it, it transforms it. It means conformity to the Son. He laid down His life for others and everyone who is a true overcomer has, without thought, laid down his or her life for the Lord and for the rest, not just for the elite, but for the whole family. Surely, we want to be like that. And when we see that, I think it cuts out all the big ideas that sometimes go along with this matter.

Do you know what God said of Abraham? It is one of the most moving things that I think that God has ever said to a man, "In thee shall all the families of the earth be blessed." If that is overcoming, I want to be an overcomer. If it means that through my life, through my way with God, through allowing God to do a work in me all the families of the earth are blessed, I think that is wonderful. Then give us a life of one hundred years without any seed, give us a life of trial and tribulation if it means that in the end all the families of the earth will be blessed. And that is what God does with the overcomer. He puts them into trials that no one else has. He allows them to go into situations that no one else faces. Challenges come to them that no one else faces. Why? It is because they are being trained in divine government, learning deeply the principles of divine government.

Where are you in this matter? It matters not where you turn in the whole Bible, you will find it all the way through. When the majority failed, God takes up one or two, or a few, or a remnant, and then He puts those people through it in such a way that in the end they come out and the rest come into the blessing.

When the few went back from Babylon to the promised land, they were a small, despised, derided people. But in the end, when the temple was built, and Jerusalem was built, and Bethlehem was rebuilt, and the cities of Galilee were rebuilt, the Scriptures could be fulfilled and the whole nation came into the blessing of the remnant. So it will be in the end when God can get a people who are prepared to move with Him and allow Him to do something in them. In the end, the whole blessing for the whole church can finally be given because God has got in some that maturity, that capacity, that being brought to the place of divine government. No wonder the apostle Paul says, "The whole creation groaneth and travaileth together in pain until now, waiting for the liberty and the glory of the sons of God." When God can get that, then the end will come. Let us praise the Lord and just commit ourselves to Him.

THE FAITH THAT OVERCOMES

Abraham

The original purpose of God in creating mankind was that man should rule and reign, should administer the government of God. In union with God, man should take that position of sovereign power over all the things God created. It is very interesting that God planted a garden and placed man in it. It was there that man was told to dress or cultivate, and keep or guard, watch, observe, care for the garden. Earlier God had told man to replenish the earth and subdue it. In other words, man was to start with the garden, learn the first lessons in dominion in the garden, and from the garden he was to go out to the whole earth. And then, what more? Surely the Lord's plan was that once man had learned dominion over natural things, physical things, and material things, in union with God, he should then go on to spiritual things and learn how to reign with God, as the New Testament says, "in the heavenlies."

Now we know man fell. We know there is no difference, no distinction; all have sinned and fallen short of the glory of God. Instead of man having dominion, things have dominion over man. Man is, himself, now not above but underneath. He is possessed by the physical, possessed by the material, governed by the natural. He is, himself, a slave. He is not having dominion over all things; he is not reigning and ruling. But the wonderful thing is, God gave to us the Lord Jesus Christ as the second Man and the last Adam, and IN HIM we see God's complete answer to this whole mess. In the Lord Jesus we see someone in union with the Father, doing all things from the Father in Him, really working the works of the Father, speaking the words of the Father, doing the will of the Father, reigning in all things above the things of time and sense and ruling even the things that are unseen and invisible.

It is a wonderful picture we have of the Lord Jesus as Man, in union with His Father, reigning and ruling. Long before He came to the right hand of the Majesty on high, long before He took the throne of God as His rightful place, before God enthroned Him at His right hand and gave all authority and power into His hand both in heaven and on earth, Jesus was ruling. In His character, in His spirit, in Himself, He was being trained. The Bible says He was perfected through sufferings, that is, He learned obedience through the things which He suffered; not that He was imperfect, but He came to the full place of maturity. Even if mankind had never sinned, still there would have been the need of training. Do you think that just because a person is pure and sinless they can sit on a throne and govern a whole portion of the universe? Not at all. That is only the beginning of the matter. Once you have dealt with sin and a person knows forgiveness, and something of holiness, and something of walking with God, you have got to train him. He has to go through situations which enable him to have an understanding as to how to rule. A person can learn the theory of reigning and ruling from a book, but it is only when you begin to face those situations in practical circumstances that you really learn to reign and rule.

I remember years ago a lady who was the finest children's nurse or health inspector in the whole area. Everyone spoke of her. When anyone was in any trouble they called her in and she gave all the advice. She was an unmarried lady, but she was able to tell them exactly what they should do and was always very helpful. Later on she got married, and believe it or not she had her own baby. Then the whole thing went to pieces. The one who in every way had been the perfect helper and advisor and counselor, just went to pieces. She kept saying at the time, "You see, it seems to be different."

People have the idea that just because you are saved and have been brought into a union with God in Christ, just because you are walking with God and know what it is to be justified, then willy-nilly you will be able to sit on a throne and govern in the kingdom that is to come. It is nonsense! That is why God's choicest saints go through the most inexplicable sufferings. You look through church history or look around you. You will find that those who are marked out because of their desire to go the whole way with God, those who really have seen this matter, have things come into their lives that are totally inexplicable. Circumstances come to them that just cannot be explained on the natural. Neither can they be explained spiritually, apart from this fact that God wants the very highest and best for that person and is prepared to bring them into situations which they cannot understand, in which their only way through is in union with God. Sometimes they have no explanation, but in union with God they go right through the situation and they come out on top.

Here is a most wonderful thing: when God does something like that in a person's life, it is forever. You never lose it. It is one of the most wonderful things that God can do, that if you go on with Him you never lose what He has given you in a dark place. It is eternal treasure. It has gone into the city. It is part of that gold, precious stone or pearl out of which that city, the bride of the Lamb is being produced. It is eternal. Often, we tend to think of the city on the intimate side of just blessed union and intimacy with Christ. We forget that a city is a center of government, a center of administration, a center of life, where everything is administered. That is why God calls the bride of Christ a city, because it is a place of government. God, at last has not only got the bride for His Son, which is wonderful in itself, but He has found someone who, in union with His Son, is able to administer the divine government in all the ages that are to come.

Do not think that this little age or two of time is everything. There are the ages of the ages. Just think of that. Do you think this last age of two thousand years has been too much? Well, you just wait for the ages of the ages. And yet, in this little age in which we are, if we cannot learn to reign here, to get on top here in Christ, we will certainly not be able to reign there. That is the dilemma God has.

When we look all the way through Scripture, we find that Christ is the sum, the basis, the heart and the circumference of all the work of God. He is Alpha and Omega, beginning and end, the first and the last and everything. God's aim is to sum up all things in Christ.

> *Unto a dispensation of the fulness of the times, to sum up all things in Christ, the things in the heavens, and the things upon the earth. (Ephesians 1:10)*

> *Where there cannot be Greek and Jew, circumcision and uncircumcision, barbarian, Scythian, bondman, freeman; but Christ is all, and in all. (Colossians 3:11)*

That is God's aim. Whether you begin at Genesis or go to Revelation you find the whole Bible is summed up in Christ. Then you find that God has redeemed a people. This mankind that God vested so much in, that fell into sin, that was alienated from God, that has become constitutionally such a different thing than what God intended it to be, has been reconciled to Himself through Christ. God has saved them, made them one with Himself, and now He wants to bring them to the place where they reign, not only in the eternity to come, but now on earth. He wants that church of His to rule in a community, to rule in a society, to sway things nationally and internationally, to dictate the course of events, to see that the will of God is done on earth as it is in heaven. It is not that He wants us to be presumptuous or arrogant and get ourselves uncovered, as many people do in prayer in this matter, but rather, in union with Christ, under the headship of Christ, in a sensitive, reverent fear of the Lord, to really govern things for God in the name of Christ.

Now that is the purpose of God, but we know very well that wherever we turn in the whole Bible we find that the majority always failed. Every time God starts with something it is wonderful and glorious and marvelous, and before a generation or two is passed, it slides away. Then what does God do? He takes up a man, or two men, or a small group, a remnant, and through that one or two, or that remnant, He does something into which He brings all the others. I call it an advance working party. They are harbingers. Originally the word *harbinger* meant someone who went ahead to find the lodgings. That is really what the overcomer is. The overcomer is not someone who says, "I am really something." That is not overcoming; that is a kind of superiority. The people who originally saw it were not superior in any way. Unfortunately one of the side effects of this teaching has been to produce a kind of atmosphere of the elite, a superior group, an inner circle group. My dear friend, there is no such thing in the kingdom of heaven.

The four and twenty elders exist to serve us and anyone who is in the government of God, whoever it is, exists for us. They will lay down their life for us. They have proved it. Most of them have laid down their life for us. As far as we know, all but one of those early twelve apostles laid down their lives for the church. The whole point is that they are only there because they have proved they can lay down their life, not once, but again and again and again. There is no idea of superiority. Not at all. They are there in order to serve you and the only idea they have in that position and ministry is to be able to serve the whole body of Christ and to serve the Lamb and the Lord God.

We find some of the elements of overcoming in the lives of different men in the Bible. One of the first great lives, the fountainhead of almost everything in the Bible, is Abraham. Abraham teaches us one thing about the overcomer. Do you remember what God said to him? "In thee shall all the families of the earth be blessed." There was nothing about being elite. God selected Abraham. The God of glory appeared unto our father, Abraham, while he was yet in Mesopotamia, in Ur of the Chaldees, and said, "Get thee out." God was going to make that man a forerunner, a pioneer, an advance working party. He established a principle in the life of Abraham that was never again to be lost in the work of God, that meant that forever afterwards the people of God would enter into something that God did in Abraham. And that is what happens with every overcomer. God establishes something in their life, something in their fellowship together. He manifests Himself; He lays a foundation that is never again taken away.

Faith

> *For whatsoever is begotten of God overcometh the world: and this is the victory that hath overcome the world, even our faith. And who is he that overcometh the world, but he that believeth that Jesus is the Son of God? (I John 5:4-5)*

The supreme thing about Abraham is his faith. Notice that this is not "*who*soever is born of God," but "*what*soever is born of God overcometh the world." It is perfectly true to say, "Whosoever is born of God overcometh the world" in one sense. But remember, "whatsoever" is very important because it means that if you are going to overcome, if you are going to rule and reign with Christ, **it must be of God.** Everything in your life must be of God. Its origin must be of God. There can be no flesh, no self-manufactured Christianity, no self-produced service and none of your own conceptions. It will all be destroyed when God starts to work with you. You have to begin with God. That is exactly what God did with Abraham.

The Land

The whole meaning of Abraham's life was the land. God said, "Into a land that I will show you." However, in the whole of his life, he never possessed an inch of that land, except the parcel of ground called Machpelah in Hebron where he buried his wife Sarah and where he, himself, was buried. That was the only portion. He spent his whole life, 175 years, wandering around doing nothing. What did he have to show for it?

Now that is what we all want to ask people: "What do you have to show for your life? What do you have to show for your faith? What tremendous success do you have? Show us, show us. We want to know. If you have faith, we want to see it."

Not Abraham! If you had quizzed Abraham and said, "Now Abraham, where are all the lives that have found God through you?"

He might have said, "I do not know any, just my family. We have even kicked Hagar out. She was the only Egyptian among us and we have kicked her out and Ishmael."

"Well," you might say, "Abraham, that is very strange. God said that in thee all the families of the earth shall be blessed. It does not look as if anyone has been blessed."

It must have been very tough for Abraham. He must have wondered whether it would be better to go back to Ur of the Chaldees and get an evangelistic mission going. Surely he must have thought, "Somehow, I must have misunderstood the mind of God. He called me out and said, 'In thee shall all the families of the earth be blessed,' and I do not have a thing to show for it. Where is this land that He told me He would give me? He said to look as far as you can to the north, and the east, and the south, and the west, and all this will I give thee." Abraham died and never saw a bit of it except what he bought with cash, just a little plot.

The City

For he looked for the city which hath the foundations,
whose builder and maker is God. (Hebrews 11:30)

Another thing that sums up the life of Abraham was the question of the city. During Abraham's whole life, he never lived in a city. The only time he ever lived in a city was Ur of the Chaldees and God told him to get out of it.

Now if you had said, "Abraham, let's get this clear. 'By their fruits ye shall know them.' You say you are looking for this city. You must be crazy. You have been living many, many years. It is not just ten years, Abraham. We'll give you ten years, but if you do not show some of the goods in ten years' time, we really begin to question. Where is this city that you have gone out to look for? You are living in tents, looking for a city. We do not understand it."

His Seed

The third thing about Abraham's life was his seed. God told him, "In thy seed shall all the families of the earth be blessed." But Abraham had no seed except Ishmael, and they kicked him out. When a man gets to ninety-nine years of age, you would think perhaps he must be a little deluded. Abraham had no seed. If he had had twelve children, or if he had had the normal number of children that they had in those days, we could have said, "Well, it is one of them, of course we see it. Even so, we wonder how all the earth is going to be blessed, Abraham, since no one yet seems to be blessed through you." But he did not have a son when he was ninety-nine years old and when Sarah was ninety. That takes some believing in a person!

What God was proving is this: "Whatsoever is born of God overcometh the world." There was something that God had revealed to Abraham which apprehended him, which gripped him. Although he had nothing to show for it, no physical or material success, he was gripped by something which God had shown him. He had a vision of God, a revelation of the Lord Jesus Christ to his own heart and he could not go back on it. Even when he fell into sin and went into

Egypt, still he went back and built the altar where he had originally departed from the Lord.

Again, when he succumbed to common sense and conceived a child through Hagar, the Egyptian, which was a curse in many ways upon his life to this day, yet, he could not ever forsake the Lord. He had seen something. Ishmael may have looked very much like his father, but the problem was, he was not born of God. He was born of common sense, the flesh, the wisdom of this world, and it could not overcome the world. Paul says in Galatians 4:30, "Cast him out, the bondwoman and her son cannot inherit the promises." It is a hard word isn't it?

You can have a beautiful facade of Christianity, a beautiful facade of service and of many other things, but if it is not of God, if its origin is not in God, it cannot overcome. One of the most difficult things for all of us is to come to the place where we say to God, "Lord, I want to be one of these overcomers by Thy grace, whatever it costs me." And then God starts to blow up the facade. We go through almost hell on earth as one after another of our facades, our projected personality, begins to disappear. For the first time, people see the kind of person we really are. But God has to start there, and if you are not prepared for that dynamiting operation, then you can never be an overcomer. "For whatsoever is begotten of God overcometh the world." In other words, it has to begin with God. Jesus is the Alpha. He must be the first letter. It is no good for you to have the A, B, C, D, and E and then letting the Lord Jesus come in on F and G. He has got to be the A and the Z. He has to be the whole thing. He has to be the first and the last, the beginning and the end. He has to be the whole. There is no other way.

Abraham did not get big ideas of empire building. He did not have great ideas of ruling Britannia, and all that kind of pomp and glory. God kept him very humble. Having shown him something born of God, something that was the purpose of God for his life and for his seed, God established in Abraham's life a principle that is infallible, as far as ruling and reigning: *everything must begin with God.* My service must begin with God. I must be called of God. I must be qualified by God. Whatever other training I have, I must know a training by the Spirit of God. "Whatsoever is born of God overcometh the world."

Then you see another thing here, "This is the victory that has overcome the world, even our faith." Once something is born of God, our hands have to be kept off it. It is one thing to see something born of God, then the next minute saying, "How can we get this thing going now? How can we really get it off the ground? Now we will get it worked out. We will do it now. This is really of God. This is absolutely the Lord. We are going to come right in behind it and we are going to see this thing get through."

This is the lesson of Abraham having to offer up Isaac. God said to Abraham, "Go up to Mount Moriah and offer up Isaac." Just think what anyone counseling Abraham might have said: "Abraham, it must be the enemy. God never asks you to sacrifice your son. Furthermore, you waited until you were one hundred years old for him to be born, do you mean to tell me that now God is saying, 'Kill him?' It cannot be God."

But Abraham overcame by faith. The Word says, "By faith Abraham, being tried, offered up Isaac. . . accounting that God is able to raise up, even from the dead" (Hebrews 11:17a, 19a). In other words, he was convinced that God's Word would come true, that whatever happened God would take responsibility. Now that is faith; faith to see a thing begin and faith to keep our hands off it all the way through so that we do not destroy it.

No man or woman will ever come to their place in the divine administration unless they are men and women of vision. Secondly, they must know that everything in their life is of God: "All my springs are in Thee." It is not in other brothers or sisters, not in a teaching, not even in the church, not in a movement, not in any things, but in Him. Thirdly, they must be men and women of faith.

In Hebrews 11 you begin to see something concerning this whole matter. Here we have all the great advance parties of history, all the harbingers of history, all the pioneers, the forerunners, the overcomers of history.

By faith Abraham, when he was called, obeyed to go out unto a place which he was to receive for an inheritance; and he went out, not knowing whither he went. By faith he became a sojourner in the land of promise, as in a land not his own, dwelling in tents, with Isaac and Jacob, the heirs with him of the same promise: for he looked for the city which hath the foundations, whose builder and maker is God. By faith even Sarah herself received power to conceive seed when she was past age, since she counted him faithful who had promised. (verses 8-11)

These all died in faith . . . (verse 13)

By faith Abraham, being tried, offered up Isaac: yea, he that had gladly received the promises was offering up his only begotten son; even he to whom it was said, In Isaac shall thy seed be called: accounting that God is able to raise up, even from the dead; from whence he did also in a figure receive him back. By faith Isaac blessed Jacob and Esau, even concerning things to come. By faith Jacob, when he was dying, blessed each of the sons of Joseph; and worshipped, leaning upon the top of his staff. By faith Joseph . . . By faith Moses . . . By faith Moses . . . (verses 17-24)

Who through faith subdued kingdoms, wrought righteousness, obtained promises, stopped the mouths of lions (verse 33). And these all, having had witness borne to them through their faith, received not the promise. (verse 39)

Therefore let us also, seeing we are compassed about with so great a cloud of witnesses, lay aside every weight, and the sin which doth so easily beset us, and let us run with patience the race that is set before us, looking unto Jesus the author and perfecter of our faith, who for the joy that was set before him endured the cross, despising shame, and hath sat down at the right hand of the throne of God. (Hebrews 12:1-2)

Here you have faith all the way through from beginning to end. Don't you find, dear child of God, that all our troubles go back to an evil heart of unbelief? If God is gracious to you this day, He will trace every one of your present problems to a lurking heart of unbelief. For instance, sometimes we say, "I don't know; I think I am being hoodwinked. Is it really worth all this discipline, all this being knocked about? Other people I know don't seem to have it. Why should I?"

You see, we can not only compare ourselves with the world, we compare ourselves with other believers. Then comes the doubt, "Is it worth it?" The interesting thing is that God never helps us. When we were little babies, God ran to help us, but once we have started the way of learning how to rule and reign, He doesn't. He will leave us; He will leave us to our thoughts, "Is it worth it? Is the end really the throne?"

Let me put it all in a nutshell. Suppose that a violent, atheistic government took our country and for the first time in many, many years believers faced persecution. Suppose the challenge was a puppet church that mouthed ethics and certain moral ideas, a conglomeration of all good men's faith. Suppose it meant that every single person who was out and out for the Lord faced either persecution, prison, death, or a life of seeming freedom. Then comes to you the question, "Is it worth it?" Would you really be prepared to die rather than deny?

Why do I ask you that question? It is because only faith could give you the victory, nothing else. You would not be able to look to circumstances; you would not be able to look to your present situation; you would not be able to look to the comfort and fellowship of your brothers and sisters since they would all be facing the same problems and perhaps separated from you. Only faith could give you the victory. And what would that faith be? It would not be some kind of faith in a set of doctrines, but it would be because you had seen something of the Lord Himself. And you could not go back; you could not deny. When you have seen something like that, the only way through is to be faithful. You overcome. I have put it in a very extreme form, but I hope that helps you. Pray God that we will not have to face such a possibility, but here you have a principle in overcoming that we call absolute faith, everything of God, a man of vision.

Why did the Lord change Abram's name to Abraham? He changed it from "exalted father" to "the father of a multitude." Dear Abraham, when he died with one son of promise and twin grandsons, he must have wondered, "Father of a multitude? Is that what God calls a multitude, three?" The point was that God was faithful. Abraham's seed would be like the sand of the seashore and like the stars of the heaven for multitude because God was establishing in Abraham a lesson for us all.

Do you want to reign and rule? God has put you in a humdrum job. God has given you a home. You may feel, "Is that the sphere of overcoming? Surely the sphere of overcoming is to go around the world declaring the gospel of the Lord Jesus Christ." That is not it at all. I fear that some of us who do go around the world like that are not overcoming. Very quickly we can be caught up in the whole system of things and lose the inward character. No, the sphere of overcoming is your home, with all its problems and difficulties, or your place of work, with its demands and challenges. It is our humdrum routine life as the people of God among all the very ordinary people that we are, bound together in the Lord, having to stay together, having to go on together, having to learn our lessons together. This is where we learn the lessons which are eternal. The word that our Lord said to the servant was this:

Well done, good and faithful servant: thou hast been faithful over a few things, I will set thee over many things. (Matthew 25:21)

May the Lord help us to understand those words rendered by the New English Bible in Luke 22:29: *"I vest in you the kingship which my Father vested in me."*

THE LIFE THAT OVERCOMES

Isaac

Ephesians 2:1-10—And you did he make alive, when ye were dead through your trespasses and sins, wherein ye once walked according to the course of this world, according to the prince of the powers of the air, of the spirit that now worketh in the sons of disobedience; among whom we also all once lived in the lusts of our flesh, doing the desires of the flesh and of the mind, and were by nature children of wrath, even as the rest: but God, being rich in mercy, for his great love wherewith he loved us, even when we were dead through our trespasses, made us alive together with Christ (by grace have ye been saved), and raised us up with him, and made us to sit with him in the heavenly places, in Christ Jesus: that in the ages to come he might show the exceeding riches of his grace in kindness toward us in Christ Jesus: for by grace have ye been saved through faith; and that not of your selves, it is the gift of God; not of works, that no man should glory. For we are his workmanship, created in Christ Jesus for good works, which God afore prepared that we should walk in them.

We have been looking at this matter of reigning with Christ, and there is another element that we need to consider. Those who are really going to reign with Christ have got to know *in experience* the risen power of Christ's life. In other words, it is not just the recognition of the need to have faith, nor just the possession of a living faith, but it is the exercise of a living faith that is the key. By faith, Abraham, when he was called, *obeyed* to go out. He did something. He exercised the faith that God had given him. And everyone who would know something of reigning with Christ must know a living faith.

God has illustrated some of the principles of reigning with Christ in different lives of saints in the Old Testament. The first one we looked at was Abraham and the one I want to underline here is Isaac. Isaac was a remarkable character in one way, and yet he pales into insignificance between two vivid, almost flamboyant characters, Abraham and Jacob. Both Abraham and Jacob overshadow Isaac. Dear Isaac never did anything original in his whole life. It is amazing. The one thing he did was dig wells, and the wells he dug were all the wells that his father, Abraham, had dug before him. All the way through the record you find Isaac like a valley connecting two huge mountain ranges, with Abraham on one side and Jacob on the other. Here is this lovely, open, sunlit, fertile valley that is Isaac, which connects the two. The point is that you cannot have a Jacob without an Isaac. He is the link between Abraham and Jacob, who became the father of the house of Israel. Symbolically, the one great thing we learn about Isaac in the Bible is that he had something to do with wells.

WELLS OF WATER

And Isaac digged again the wells of water, which they had digged in the days of Abraham his father; for the Philistines had stopped them after the death of Abraham: and he called their names after the names by which his father had called them. And Isaac's servants digged in the valley, and found there a well of springing water. And the herdsmen of Gerar strove with Isaac's herdsmen, saying, The water is ours: and he called the name of the well Esek, because they contended with him. And they digged another well, and they strove for that also: and he called the name of it Sitnah. And he removed from thence, and digged another well; and for that they strove not: and he called the name of it Rehoboth; and he said, For now the Lord hath made room for us, and we shall be fruitful in the land. And he builded an altar there, and called upon the name of the Lord, and pitched his tent there: and there Isaac's servants digged a well. (Genesis 26:18-22, 25)

And it came to pass the same day, that Isaac's servants came and told him concerning the well which they had digged, and said unto him, We have found water. And he called it Shibah: therefore the name of the city is Beersheba unto this day. (verse 32-33)

It is all wells of water. In the Bible, water is a symbol of life, because in desert conditions, it is water, sweet water, that makes all the difference between life and death, between barrenness and fruitfulness, between fertility and just an arid desert or wilderness.

Jesus spoke about wells, and when we come to it we make a tremendous discovery. The Christian life is not all to do with doctrines, with technique, with methods, with some institutional, traditional movement. The Christian life is all to do with being made alive together with Christ. That is *the* characteristic of the child of God.

The overcomers have within them the qualities and characteristics that every Christian ought to have. However, many do not have these characteristics because of unbelief, or sin, or backsliding. So God takes certain ones and sees to it they are a testimony; they are a witness. They not only have a living faith which they exercise, but they are also made alive together with Christ.

Jesus answered and said unto her, Every one that drinketh of this water shall thirst again: but whosoever drinketh of the water that I shall give him shall never thirst; but the water that I shall give him shall become in him a well of water springing up unto eternal life. (John 4:13-14)

It is such a sad thing when Christians become morbid, dark, heavy people because the characteristic of the child of God is eternal life, resurrection life, abundant life. It is this marvelous word of the Lord: "It shall become in him a well of water springing up unto eternal life." It is one thing to have to run off every time and go to this meeting and get a little drink, go off to that conference and get a little drink, go off to this speaker and get a little drink; but, it is another thing to have the well inside. When you have the well inside, that makes all the difference in the world because you have something which springs up. It is not just an automatic supply in the sense that it is always the same level. It springs up. There are times when the water does not spring up quite the same in you. It is quieter. There are other times when it springs up, but it is inside of you. Think of that! The life is right inside you. The Spirit of God has brought the source of eternal life into your being, into your house of clay, into this funny little vessel that we all have, inside these bodies that we have with us in their various states and conditions. If we are children of God, we have the heart of the matter brought into us: "Made alive together with Christ."

Some Christians are so miserable, so dark, so heavy. You would think that everything in the world is against them. In fact they say so, "Oh, it is hard being a Christian. It is a difficult thing to become a Christian, especially today when it is not popular. People sneer at you. They laugh at you. The whole current of the world is against you. You have obstacles no one else has to face. You have an antagonism that no one else has."

Of course you have! The only time in church history that you did not really have it was in the Victorian Era. Think of those early Christians who were fed to the lions. That is some obstacle. Do you think that it was easy to become a child of God at the very beginning when the whole world was against them? They went to their death with laughter in their mouths. They went to their death, again and again, with joy and absolute faith in God.

We have a little book which is called *The Mirror of Sufferers* in which are recorded the last words of some of those who died under that evil woman, Bloody Queen Mary. Hundreds of them were burned at the stake. Those stories are all in the old English and record the words actually taken down at the time by eyewitnesses. It was an incredible thing that people could go to their death with such joy because they had seen the Lord. They had been made alive together with Christ. *That* is the characteristic of the Christian life.

Only a dead fish floats with the current. A live fish uses the current to go upstream, uses it to face incredible torrents and rapids and strong currents. The life is so constituted that it can use the very current flowing against it to go up. And that is exactly what happens to the child of God. Once he or she discovers the fulness of Christ's life, the power of eternal life, the power of His resurrection, they have a key which means that the very afflictions, problems, antagonisms, and obstacles are used to advance that person in the Lord. Instead of destroying them, it perfects them; instead of bringing them underneath, it brings them out on top; instead of making them miserable and empty and unhappy, they come out reigning with Christ. Through many tribulations we must enter into the kingdom of God!

MADE ALIVE WITH CHRIST

Of course you can say, "Oh dear, dear, dear, it is so difficult to be a Christian." Why not put the emphasis on the other foot? What about the fact that you have been made alive together with Christ? The world does not have that. Look at what a miserable world it is! I made a list of some of the things we heard this week: one person shot in the stomach, a person machine-gunned down, a bomb in Lisbon, a bomb in Paris, a bomb in Belfast, a bomb somewhere else. It is a most miserable world to live in. We never hear about any joyful, happy things anymore. It is just one long list of misery. But the child of God has something that the worldling does not have. He has been made alive together with Christ. When Christ was raised, he was brought into the very power of His resurrection.

Listen to the words of the apostle Paul as he prays for the Ephesian Christians that God may give to them a spirit of wisdom and revelation in the knowledge of Christ:

And what the exceeding greatness of his power to usward who believe, according to that working of the strength of his might which he wrought in Christ, when he raised him from the dead, and made him to sit at his right hand in the heavenly places, far above all rule, and authority, and power, and dominion, and every name that is named, not only in this world, but also in that which is to come. (Ephesians 1:19-21)

Then he goes on to say in chapter 2, "You did he make alive together with Christ and raised up together with Christ and made to sit together with Christ in heavenly places." Therefore, if anyone is to know anything about overcoming or fulfillment of the purpose of God, he must know the life of Christ. If you are not a Christian, if you have never tasted of the salvation of God, that is where you must begin, by receiving Christ as the life of God. When He steps into your life, you can sing, "Christ liveth in me. Oh, what a salvation is this, that Christ liveth in me." Then you can have all the obstacles and antagonism this world can think of, you can have all the strong current flowing against you, but you have a life inside of you that will not rest until it has got you home.

You have a life inside you that is constituted for problems. Did you realize that? You see, we think of ourselves. We rush to our own wisdom, our own strength, our own resources, our own grit, our own courage, and in the end it breaks down. We fail to recognize as believers that we have been constituted for catacomb life. We have been constituted for persecution. We have been constituted to stand against the flow of things in this world, including unpopularity and all the other things that come with the inexplicable. We have a life this world does not have.

Do you think it was easy for the Lord Jesus Christ when He endured the gainsaying and contradiction of sinners? Do you think that it was easy for Him to bear the malice and hatred of the establishment in the nation? Do you think that it was easy for Him to bear all their plotting, their cunning, their cleverness, their insinuations and all the rest of it? Of course not! Jesus, Himself, stood against the current of this world and fulfilled the purpose of God. And once we allow THE OVERCOMER to get into us, we start to know what it is to gain the victory. This is a tremendous matter!

Sometimes when we hear this term, *victory*, we tend to think that it is when there is not a breath of trouble anywhere. We think that victory is when everything is marvelous and we are smiling and triumphant and full of praise. Years ago, I asked an older brother who knew very much about this thing, "What do you call victory?"

He thought for a few moments and then he said, "Victory is to be still on course at the end of your life." What a wonderful way to put it! It does not mean that you haven't been knocked down, that you did not flag or stumble, that there were no times when you nearly got out of the race. But overcoming victory is that by the grace of God, by the life of Christ inside of you, by the Spirit of Christ within, you come right through and end on course. "Made alive together with Christ."

THE LAW OF THE SPIRIT OF LIFE

There is a hymn that says: "As in the cone, the seed." Many of you have been in mountain areas and seen the pine trees there. If I had in my hand the cone of one of those pine trees, you would be able to see it very well. But what if I had the seed from inside the cone in my hand? You would think, "Look at that little black thing there in the palm of his hand. It does not look like much life in there. It is nothing but a shriveled up, dried up, insignificant, weak little bit of chaff."

But if you take that little piece of chaff and drop it into a crack or fissure in a huge boulder, many, many tons in weight, and if some damp gets down there, under the right conditions, that little bit of chaff germinates. What happens? If you could see it, you would surely laugh. Two little white threads would go down, and then another little white thread would go down, the weakest, stupidest, silliest little things in the whole world. Then two little green shoots would come out the top. If you could talk to it you would say, "You silly little thing. Do you really think that you can overcome this boulder? Do you think that you are going to become a pine tree? You do not even look like a pine tree."

If you have seen a little pine seedling at the beginning, it does not look the least bit like a pine tree, does it? You might say to it, "Oh, you are kidding yourself. You must have been hallucinating. Do you really think that you are going to grow and live?"

But as those little roots go down into the fissure of the rock and somehow or other get the nutrition that they need, and as that little stem goes up, slowly it becomes a sapling, and in the end it becomes a tree. It grows up into the sunlight, into the heavens, and what happens? It splits the boulder! If you had asked me what the odds were against that little sapling living or that little piece of chaff ever germinating, I would have had to say that the odds must be colossal against it. How can a little piece of chaff do anything against a boulder tons in weight? Why, if you think about it, it is ridiculous. Yet there are many examples of this in mountain areas—the huge boulder lying shattered, and in the midst of it a magnificent tree.

Where did it all begin? Some people will say, "Well, if a tree got dropped out of heaven like that, I can see that it could be a possibility. Lightning might have struck the rock in a miracle and the thing shattered. Then this magnificent tree just appeared."

But it did not begin like that. *That* is the miracle of it. The little bit of dried-up brown chaff that was a seed out of a cone had life in it, and once it learned to obey the law of its life, that is all it needed. It did not need some great mechanical bulldozer or stone crusher. It did not have to say to someone else, "Crush this stone for me. I cannot live without your help. Crush it."

No! All it had to do was obey the life that was in it. It is ridiculous. How can a little seed that size overcome a boulder nearly half the size of a room? That is impossible. But if it obeys the law of its life, it happens. That is the wonderful thing about being a child of God.

Some people come to me and say, "This is all a wonderful theory and a marvelous ideal, but for me, it is impossible. You don't know my family background. Oh, I have the most impossible family you have ever seen."

Now I have lived long enough to find that there are an incredible number of these impossible families. Indeed, it seems that nearly everybody has some impossible relative. Because of some impossible background they say, "I would love to become a Christian. I would love to know the fulness of Christ, but it is impossible for me. You do not understand my problems. I have inherited weaknesses. I have inherited family problems. There are flaws in my temperament, spots on my personality, and I do not know what to do about it."

My dear friend, if God has put within you the Lord Jesus Christ, He is sufficient for your family weaknesses no matter *what* they are. If you will only learn to *obey the law of the Spirit of life in Christ Jesus,* you will grow out of all your problems. The real problem is that we do not put the emphasis upon the law of the Spirit of life in Christ Jesus. We put it on ourselves.

Other people come to me and say that they have great problems and difficulties. Things have gone wrong in their lives. Circumstances have now come into their lives which are irrevocable, which cannot be changed. They say it is like a great boulder that shuts out the sunlight of heaven. It is like something sitting on top of them. "It is no good. It is not for me," they say.

But it is the only answer to their problem. No doctor can answer it. No psychiatrist can answer it. No social reformer can answer it. No one can answer it. Not even religion can answer it. The only answer to your problem is the life of Christ. If you let the living Christ into your life, once you obey Him, follow Him and do what He wants, you experience His life more and more and you grow in Him. Then, almost unknowingly, the boulder begins to be split as you grow. And there will come a day when that boulder will lie shattered all around you, and you will be a stately tree in the house of the Lord, in the courts of the Lord. It is a wonderful thing what God can do!

Let me use an illustration. There are times when I sit in a jumbo jet, and being someone who has no understanding of these matters, wonder how it will ever get off the ground. The last time I was in a jumbo jet, every single seat was filled up and some of them were large people. There was all the food for two meals for a transatlantic flight. Then there was all the luggage for four hundred people. (I thought, "If everyone has as much luggage as I have, what a weight!") Outside the window there was an engine in which I could stand up inside and that was only one of four engines. How does this thing really get off the ground with four hundred people, all the cabin crew, the pilots, all the meals and all the luggage?

If I went out on the runway and ran as fast as I could and flapped my wings, I would not get off the ground because there is the law of gravity. If I ran as fast as the fastest sprinter, still I would not get up into the air, even if I had some kind of wings attached to my arms. The law of gravity would be too much for me. I know some people who drive furiously. Even if they were to get their car on the runway and go as fast as they could, they would not leave the ground. Maybe they would leave the ground for a moment, but they would come down again. How could this plane ever get off the ground?

The law of gravity is the one law I know. It is a good illustration because most of us know only one law morally, the law of sin and death. We do not know any other law: "The things we would, we do not, and the things we would not, those things we do." We all know the law of sin and death. It is as strong as the law of gravity. It pulls us down.

So we say, "I know what I will do. I will read the Bible for five days on end." We are exhausted at the end of it. We get quite a bit of biblical knowledge, but then comes a temptation and we are down.

So we say, "Ah, I will spend the day in prayer and fasting." We spend a whole day in prayer and fasting. We spend a whole day without food. Think of that! At the end of it we feel wonderful. We go to bed, get up the next morning, find a temptation, and we are down. It is the law of sin and death.

Then we say, "I know what it is. I need to know more fellowship." So we rush out and get as much fellowship as we possibly can in two months. Along comes temptation and we are down.

The law of sin and death is too much for us. It is like the law of gravity. We cannot get rid of it. Some of us try to suppress it. Now to me, suppressing the law of sin and death is rather like a lilo or an air mattress. When you push it down here, it comes up there. You cannot get rid of it. If you push it down here, the air cannot get out. It can only come up somewhere else. So you push it down there and it is up here. Then you push it down there. That is what some people try to do with the law of sin and death in their lives. They spend their whole time pushing it down until they are absolutely miserable. No wonder Christians are down and depressed and empty and look heavy. They say, "Being a Christian is so difficult. It is full of sorrow." No wonder there is no life.

But listen! When that jumbo jet gets on the runway, starts its engines, and the full thrust of the power is there, it begins to run along. Finally it starts to go up and up and up, and it is into the heavens. A superior law has taken over from the law of gravity. That is the only way that you and I will ever know deliverance from the law of sin and death. As it says in Romans 8:2: "For the law of the Spirit of life in Christ Jesus made me free from the law of sin and of death."

The law of the Spirit of life in Christ Jesus is a superior law. We are made alive together with Christ, knowing the power of His life inside; knowing something of His care, His faithfulness, His provision, His energy, His resources inside of us. Then we find that we are free from the law of sin and death. Oh, how wonderful it is!

Dear Isaac is the illustration of this lesson for us. Isaac received and passed on. It is such a simple lesson. Isaac was not a flamboyant personality; he was not one of those vivid characters, and yet God was teaching us one great lesson through his life. If you and I want to know the life of Christ, we must learn to be a vessel, and we must learn to be a receiver.

How do we know this life? We receive the life. We do not have it in ourselves. We have to receive the Lord, and then we have to know what it is to grow in that life and let that life grow more and more in us.

Jesus said, "I am come that they may have life and that they may have life more abundantly" (John 10:10). That is wonderful. He did not say, "I am come that you might have eternal life when you die, but now you have a miserable existence down here facing all the problems and difficulties and obstacles. Then one day when you die, you will get eternal life." He said, "I am come that ye may have life and that ye may have life more abundantly."

John, the apostle, put it like this: "He that hath the Son hath the life; he that hath not the Son of God hath not the life" (I John 5:12). In John 7:37-38 Jesus said: "If any man thirst, let him come unto Me and drink. He that believeth on Me, as the scripture hath said, from within him shall flow rivers of living water."

LAUGHTER

This well springing up unto life eternal is the most wonderful thing because it becomes rivers of living water for other people. No wonder God said to Abraham, "When the season comes around, your wife will bear a son."

Abraham fell on the ground and laughed. And God said to him, "Abraham, it is so. It shall come to pass. And you shall call your son, Isaac, because it means *laughter*."

When that boy was born, Sarah said, "God hath made me to laugh; every one that heareth will laugh with me" (Genesis 21:6).

There is a laughter about this life. Oh yes, Christians are the only people who can afford to really laugh. No wonder it says in Psalm 35: "They shall return to Zion with laughter in their mouths." They are the only people who can afford to laugh. How can you laugh when you are on the broad way to hell? How can you laugh if you are a child of God and living in the world, if you are compromised with one foot in the world and one foot in the kingdom of God? But if you really belong to the Lord Jesus Christ, let the obstacles come, let the difficulties come, let the antagonism come, you have a laughter. You are an Isaac. You see, what happens to the world is to nothing, but what happens to the Christian is to glory. A tragedy in a worldling's life brings nothing. There is no meaning. However, a tragedy in a believer's life brings glory because through it, he learns to reign and rule.

Have you ever noticed that wonderful little phrase in Romans 5:17? It is one of those phrases that is buried in a theological passage that I think most people miss.

For if, by the trespass of the one, death reigned through the one; much more shall they that receive the abundance of grace and of the gift of righteousness reign in life through the one, even Jesus Christ.

The world knows death reigning over them—corruption, futility, emptiness. But the child of God, through the work of the Lord Jesus, can know what it is to reign in life through Jesus Christ.

Are you an Isaac? I do not know where you stand, whether you are a child of God or not. If you are not a Christian, God can speak to you about life, about knowing the gift of God which is eternal life through Jesus Christ our Lord. Don't you want to? For me, it is the most wonderful thing in the whole world. That is the thing the Christian has that the Hindu, or the Buddhist, or the Muslim, or the Confucianist does not have. Ethics? Yes. Morality? Yes. Decency? Yes. Much else? Yes. But the one thing the Christian has is this: he or she has been made alive together with Christ.

Maybe there are others of you who are Christians, but you do not know too much about life. Sin is hampering your way with God. Something is holding you back, something is fettering you. You want to know the fulness of His life and the power of His life. God can meet with you. May the Lord in His mercy and love meet every need.

OVERCOMING THE SELF-LIFE

Jacob

Luke 22:29-30—And I appoint unto you a kingdom, even as my Father appointed unto me, that ye may eat and drink at my table in my kingdom; and ye shall sit on thrones judging the twelve tribes of Israel.

And now I vest in you the kingship which my Father vested in me; you shall eat and drink at my table in my kingdom and sit on thrones as judges of the twelve tribes of Israel. (New English Bible)

Luke 12:32—Fear not, little flock; for it is your Father's good pleasure to give you the kingdom. (In the original, "kingdom" is primarily an abstract noun denoting sovereign or royal power and authority. It then came to mean concretely, the territory and people ruled over.)

Matthew 16:19—I will give unto thee the keys of the kingdom of heaven: and whatsoever thou shalt bind on earth shall be bound in heaven; and whatsoever thou shalt loose on earth shall be loosed in heaven.

Revelation 3:21—He that overcometh, I will give to him to sit down with me in my throne, as I also overcame, and sat down with my Father in his throne.

Revelation 2:26-28—And he that overcometh, and he that keepeth my works unto the end, to him will I give authority over the nations: and he shall rule them with a rod of iron, as the vessels of the potter are broken to shivers; as I also have received of my Father: and I will give him the morning star.

In this matter of having dominion or reigning with Christ, the lives of the saints in the Old Testament are full of instruction. Through each one, as recorded, the Lord has revealed and illustrated essential characteristics of kingship, or overcoming, or having dominion. We must never forget that the overcomer is God's norm, not His especial, and that is where most people make their great mistake. They think the overcomer is some kind of elite, whereas the overcomer, as we find it in the Word of God, is really God's norm. The overcomer is the normal child of God, the normal servant of the Lord, the servant of the Lord as God designed him and intended him to be. However, in days of decline, days of backsliding, days of sin and unbelief and compromise, then there is a remnant that God uses because they are ready to go on with Him. He can take them on as forerunners or harbingers or the advance working party. They are those who go before and prepare the ground for the rest. They follow the Lord the whole way and become the means by which the rest enter into blessing.

I want to take up the life of Jacob which is a most wonderful illustration of this principle of kingship. Reigning with Christ is not only a matter of absolute faith, as found in the life of Abraham, and divine resurrection life and power, as found in the life of Isaac. Jacob, in many ways, is meant to be the completion of what God began in Abraham. He began something in Abraham, continued and developed it in Isaac, and he wanted to complete it in Jacob. That is why forever afterwards God is known as the God of Abraham, of Isaac and of Jacob. It is as if these three together somehow represent the most vital aspect of overcoming or of reigning with Christ.

JACOB BY NATURE

The problem with Jacob was the strength of his own self-life. This is a perennial problem, and if you have not met it yet, you have not gone very far along the Christian way. We can have real faith and a real experience of the life of God, but the problem which faces us sooner or later is the strength of our own self-life. We know what God wants and what the purpose of God is. We have begun to see something. We have an understanding of what the Lord is driving at; and furthermore, we have an experience of life. But the thing that gets us down again and again is the strength of our own will.

We find that we have a stubbornness, an obstinacy, and areas in our lives that will not yield. We know what we should do, we know the issues that should be settled, but we will not do it. God has taken Jacob to illustrate and reveal once and for all time the need for us to be delivered from the strength of our own self-life.

The self-life manifests itself in many differing ways. In one person it can be self-righteousness. In another person it can be swindling, as with Jacob. In another person it can be a kind of obstinacy that will not yield. It manifests itself in all different ways in different people, and of course, the stronger the personality the greater the problem.

By nature, Jacob was not a prince with God, nor was he one who blessed others, nor was he a worshiper. This man, far from being a prince with God, was a bargainer with God. Every time the Lord appeared to Jacob he immediately struck a bargain. It is a most incredible story.

Do you remember that tremendous encounter he had with God when he ran away from home and fled from his twin brother, Esau? He laid down and went to sleep with a stone for a pillow. There he had that dream where he saw a ladder going up from earth to heaven and angels ascending and descending. Above the ladder he saw the Lord, Himself, standing. When he woke up he said, "This place is a terrible place." It was called Luz, but he said, "I will call it Bethel, the house of God, for this is the house of God. This is none other than the gate to heaven."

Then the Lord appeared to him. He built an altar and said, "Lord, if You will bring me back to this place, I will build You a house." At that point the Lord was not overly interested in anyone building Him a house. That was to come later with Moses. He wanted something else, but Jacob could not help himself. He did not bow down to the ground and worship the Lord. He did not prostrate himself before the Lord. There was no worship. He said, "Lord, if You do this and this, then You, the Lord, will be my God and I will build You a house on this place." Wasn't that kind of him? God never wanted a house built for Him in Bethel; He wanted it in Jerusalem. Later on, when Israel parted from Judah, they built a house of the Lord in Bethel which was an abomination in the eyes of the Lord and one of the causes for the wrath of the prophets. This is the strength of our natural life.

Think how thrilled you would be if you saw, in vision, a staircase going from the earth to heaven and angels going up and down. Most of us would be thrilled if we saw one angel, but to see all those angels crowding up and down. You would have been thrilled to see communication between heaven and earth, and the Lord standing beside that ladder as if saying, "I want heaven and earth to be one."

Jacob saw something, but then the strength of his natural life came out, and he said, "Lord, You revealed something to me. It is obvious You want something of me. Now, if you bring me back here, You shall be my God and I will build You a house right on this spot." There are thousands of so-called churches built just in that way. All kinds of Christian work is done just like that. Half of it is real vision and the other half is the strength of our natural life and worldly wisdom. Jacob was not a prince with God. He was a bargainer with God, and you find it on two or three other occasions through the record. He bargained with God. He was not someone who blessed others. It says in Hebrews, "By faith Jacob, when he was dying, blessed each of the sons of Joseph; and worshiped, leaning upon the top of his staff" (Hebrews 11:21).

That is the wonderful last picture we have of Jacob in the Bible. He blessed people and his blessing really meant something. It was not just a few words that he uttered in the name of the Lord. It was a real blessing; something was imparted by his blessing. Yet by nature, Jacob was not someone who could bless other people. He stole their blessings. He stole his twin brother's blessing as well as his birthright. That was Jacob's nature.

Are you like that? Are you the kind of person who cannot be let out long for fellowship because you steal things all the time and ruin anything? It is an acquisitiveness; something that just wants to have everything under its control, to manipulate it, to have a domination over it. That was Jacob. He was certainly not a worshiper; he was a swindler. For twenty-one years he swindled his uncle, and his uncle, of course, swindled him. He was not a worshiper. We do not have any record in all those years that he ever worshiped the Lord. It was not in his nature.

BECOMING A WORSHIPER

We have to ask ourselves, "Can someone who is a bargainer with God, someone who is out to get the better of God and anybody else, someone who will go to extraordinary lengths to steal both birthright and blessing from his own twin brother, ever come to the throne?"

The problem is that many people with their sweet evangelical piety could never think of themselves as Jacob because they have probably never been exposed to the kind of temptations or the kind of circumstances that could reveal what they are. Therefore they think, "Oh, of course not!" But here is the glory of the whole matter. God took the minimum, as it were, and said, "By taking Jacob I want you all to understand that no one is beyond the transforming power of the grace of God to bring them from this to that." The bargainer with God can become the prince with God. The one who steals others' blessings and birthrights can become the one who imparts blessings of real value to others. The one who was a swindler can become, in the end, a real worshiper; but, the cost will be that the strength of his natural life will be crippled forever. He will limp to the end of his days.

We do not know exactly what did happen with Jacob when he wrestled with the angel. Nearly all the modern commentators, both Jewish and Christian, consider that his hip was dislocated. Think of that! What pain that must have been! They did not know too much about manipulation in those days, so for the rest of his life he walked with a crutch or with a staff. That is why in the Hebrew the last picture we have of him is leaning on the bedpost or the end of the bed. He blessed those two boys and then he worshiped, "leaning on his staff" (Greek). Both are true, because generally speaking he could never do without his staff, but when he was in bed he did not need it. When he sat up, he did need the end of the bed to hang on to. The fact is that God did something to cripple that man in order to bring him into kingship. It is one of the most wonderful pictures in the Word of God of the grace of God and the love of God. We shall never understand these words, "Jacob have I loved but Esau have I hated." They are mysterious, essential mystery. But the fact remains and we should never forget that God somehow set His love upon Jacob. He loved him out of swindling into blessing, and out of stealing or cheating into being one who could bless others, into a prince with God.

The problem was his old nature. I do not know if you have yet discovered that is your problem. If the problem is sin we know that there is an answer to sin in the finished work of Jesus Christ. We know that the blood of Jesus Christ, God's Son, cleanses us from all sin. The second thing we know is that we must cease from sin. We cannot just continue in sin. I believe that most people will forsake sin once they have seen it in their lives and confessed it. Our problem, generally speaking, is not sins, it is self. It is that strong-willed self-life that appears when we least expect it. We go to a place and receive a great blessing, and we go away full of it. Then we find out within weeks that the old Adam has reared its ugly head once more, and we are back where we began.

> *Knowing this, that our old man was crucified with him, that the body of sin might be done away, that so we should no longer be in bondage to sin. (Romans 6:6)*

> *But ye did not so learn Christ; if so be that ye heard him, and were taught in him, even as truth is in Jesus: that ye put away, as concerning your former manner of life, the old man, that waxeth corrupt after the lusts of deceit; and that ye be renewed in the spirit of your mind, and put on the new man, that after God hath been created in righteousness and holiness of truth. (Ephesians 4:20-24)*

> *For I know that in me, that is, in my flesh, dwelleth no good thing: [Here is a Christian speaking, a child of God.] for to will is present with me, but to do that which is good is not. For the good which I would I do not: but the evil which I would not, that I practise. (Romans 7:18-19)*

We know that we should do certain things and we do not do them. Sometimes after a meeting people come to me and say, "I know that I should have gone forth," or, "I know that I ought to get this and this settled." Then there are things which we know we ought not to do and we are doing them. The problem is our self-life.

THE RENEWING OF THE MIND

And be not fashioned according to this world: but be ye transformed by the renewing of your mind, that ye may prove what is the good and acceptable and perfect will of God. (Romans 12:2)

The Authorized Version, the Revised Standard Version, and the New American Standard Bible all use the word *conformed*. "Be not conformed to the world but be ye transformed by the renewing of your mind." I think the old standard version of 1901 is a wonderful rendering that "Ye be not fashioned according to this world," molded according to this world. It is the same idea as conformed—just doing what the world does, acting like the world does, having the spirit that the world has, responding as the world responds. The Bible says, "And be not fashioned according to this world but be ye transformed by the renewing of your mind."

It is interesting that in Ephesians 4:22, speaking about the old man, it is exactly the same word, "Be renewed in the spirit of your mind." It is there that our whole problem lies. It certainly was with Jacob. He had a mind that was as sharp as sharp could be, a mind that could strike a bargain in an instant. He saw the gain and his mind worked overtime on it. He could not help himself. I am quite sure afterwards he would ask, "Oh, should I have said that to the Lord?" He could not help himself. It was his mind.

I find that the greatest problem in the Christian life is myself. Do you find this problem? I want to do the will of God. I want to follow the Lord the whole way. I know exactly what I should do. But I find that so often something in me, before I can bottle it, or get hold of it, or apprehend it, or arrest it, or imprison it, has done the thing and left me with the damage. So often we live in a kind of cloudy, cuckoo land where we do not really realize what we are or what we are doing. Once we become aware of ourselves, we suddenly find that we do these things before we hardly have time to breathe.

It is natural because it is to do with the mind. As a man thinks, so he is.

Do not be too hard on Jacob. Some people sit in great judgment of Jacob and say, "Oh, dreadful man, dreadful man!" Unfortunately, lots of others have inherited it from him. The truth is he was not such a dreadful man. He was a very astute, clever businessman. He was the kind of man who makes a million dollars easily. He saw a bargain and struck it. He could see how he could engineer things quickly and manipulate things in the right way in his estimation. Before he knew where he was, he had a million in the kitty. He was only doing what came naturally. I am quite sure that lots of people are very jealous of such people. Then it is very easy to say "swindler!" The point is, they are not too good at it. The old swindler is just as much in them, but they are not too clever.

THE WORK OF GOD'S GRACE

Jacob was a clever man, and he becomes, therefore, *the* great example of the strength of our natural man, of our self-life. There was something in Jacob that was very lovable. After all, he put a value on the birthright, and his beloved, athletic twin brother had no time for it. Jacob put a value on the blessing which his brother only dimly began to realize. Deep, deep down in him, Jacob had a heart for the Lord, but his problem was his self-life. The wonderful thing is that we see exemplified and expressed in this life of Jacob the work of God's grace. We find it most wonderfully in the New Testament:

> *For whom he foreknew, he also foreordained to be conformed to the image of his Son, that he might be the firstborn among many brethren. (Romans 8:29)*

I find that the right kind of predestination. Here is a foreordination of God concerning this child of God. God has foreordained that that one should be conformed to the image of His Son. That is the wonderful thing about Jacob. God took Jacob on because He had foreordained that Jacob should become Israel. He had foreordained that he should be conformed to the image of His Son. Somehow or other, by the sheer way that God would lead him, he would come, not only to a self-revelation and to self-despair; but in the end, he would come to the most wonderful experience of the transforming power and grace of God.

People tell me that should all come at conversion, but it does not always happen that way. I know people who have been so marvelously converted that they never needed anything else. They entered in at the beginning and just went on with the Lord. Thank God for such people. Some of us are not like them. I can only say that when the Lord met me in a deeper way later on, I hardly thought I had ever been converted in the first place. I have a feeling that Jacob would probably say something along the same line, too. The Lord was with him. He was in a relationship with God right at the beginning, but there was the strength of his own natural life in the things of God, bargaining with God, manipulating the things of God. But God met him! Jacob met his match in the Lord.

We always think the grace of God was the angel of the Lord that wrestled with him all night. But it was also the grace of God that allowed Jacob to swindle his brother out of his birthright, steal his blessing by a sheer deception, causing him to run away to the only other bigger swindler in the Middle East. Those two swindlers were locked up for just over twenty years in the same household, swindling each other until Jacob became so sick of swindling that he was ready for the angel of the Lord.

Some of us say, "Why didn't the Lord meet me years ago? Why all this waste?" My dear friend, I am afraid that you would not have responded if the Lord had met you years ago. That is the tragedy of our nature. So often we have to go all the way through this long way, and as God deals with us, finally we come to the place where we are ready for God to do something. ["Transformed by the renewing of your mind that you may prove what is the good and perfect and acceptable will of God."]

What was the will of God for Jacob? He was to become the father of the house of Israel, his name given to the people of God forever. That was the will of God for Jacob, and he was as far from it as it was possible to be. But the grace of God got to work on him.

SEEING THE LORD

*But we all, with unveiled face beholding as in a mirror
the glory of the Lord, are transformed into the same
image from glory to glory, even as from the Lord the
Spirit. (II Corinthians 3:18)*

How did Jacob get changed? He was changed when he
saw the Lord. He called it Peniel, *the face of God.* "I have
seen the face of God and I have lived." In Hebrew the word
used, *presence of the Lord,* is very much like *the face of the
Lord.* It means the same thing because in the Hebrew idea, a
person's face is his presence located. Our face is our presence.

Before Jacob could become Israel, the Lord had to bring
him to see himself. There could be no kingship or overcoming
without such a work, nor will there be with you. You will
never come to kingship, you will never overcome, until you see
yourself.

Jacob quietly swindled his uncle Laban for seven years
for the hand of his beloved younger daughter, Rachel. When
the wedding ceremony was over and they finally got away and
the veil was lifted, he found Leah. Jacob must have been
scandalized because it was the biggest swindle he had ever
known. Have you ever heard of anyone swindling a person
over marriage? That is going right down to the very bottom.

Laban and his wife must have said to Leah, "Now dear,
you keep your big mouth shut. If you as much as open your
mouth once in this whole proceeding, the game will be up. If
you want to get married, you have got to be quiet. Just stand
there under the veil and do nothing. Try to walk like your
sister, act like your sister, do everything like your sister."

I do not know what they did to dear sister, whether they
sent her off or gave her something to knock her out for a few
hours, but it is an incredible story. It is as if you can hear the
scandalized Jacob saying, "My own flesh and blood! Can you
think it is possible, under the whole sun, for my own uncle, my
mother's brother, to do this to his nephew? It is not possible.
Surely if he were a distant relative one could understand, but
he is my uncle and I have worked for seven hard years."

I don't suppose at that moment there came a whisper to his ear, "And what about your twin brother? It was not your uncle or your nephew, but your *twin* brother. You were born one minute later. You swindled him out of his birthright and out of his blessing."

Such is the delusion and strength of our self-life that we can deceive ourselves at that point to think, "How could anyone possibly do such a thing to me?" Oh, he appeared to get over it and agreed to work another seven years for his uncle Laban for dear Rachel.

As we read the story, we find they were all swindlers. Leah was in on it. She was always doing things in the home. Then you know the story of Rachel. Later, when Jacob was finally sick to death of the whole lot he said, "We will go back home. I do not care if my brother kills me. I would rather go back to my brother and face his wrath than stay a moment longer in this swindler's household."

He left for home, and two days journey out in Gilead, they suddenly saw a cloud of dust and camels coming fast down the track. What was it? It was dear old Uncle Laban with a posse of his men. They stopped them and said, "The family gods are gone!"

Jacob drew himself up to his full height and said, "The family gods! I have never ever worshiped idols, and I never want to have anything to do with them. Do you think I would take idols? Search everybody!"

Uncle Laban, who understood his nephew quite well, did just that. He searched everybody, and when he came to his beloved Rachel sitting upon the camel looking pale and weak, she said, "I am not feeling too well, Papa. You do not have to search this camel do you?"

And he said, "No, darling," and went on. Under the saddle were all the family gods. She was a swindler as well.

That was the last straw for Jacob. That night he met the Lord. It was as if his whole house collapsed around him. He had never thought that Rachel could be guilty of such a thing. He saw himself in Laban, then he saw himself in Leah, and then he saw himself in Rachel. Finally, he was ready for the angel of the Lord. And when God appeared to him and he saw the face of the Lord, then he persisted.

PERSISTENCE

Here is a most wonderful thing about Jacob, and it is true of every overcomer. You will never, never come to the throne unless you persist, unless you endure, and when your moment of opportunity comes, stay up all night. I know people who have stayed up all night and just worn themselves out. I have known people who have fasted for things to try and persuade the Lord to do something. But there comes a time in the sovereignty of God when your moment comes. If you forget it now, one day it will come back to you. When your moment comes, when God really visits you and has you in a corner, when there is no way out and you know the Lord is there, hold on to Him. Do not let Him go. The Lord loves it. It is exactly what He wants.

Forever afterwards God boasted about Jacob and said, "He would not let Me go." The prophet Hosea says, "And he strove with the Lord and would not let Him go!" Persistence! There is one rabbinical tradition that says the name Israel means, "God persists." Jacob would never have been anywhere if God had not persisted. And somehow I think God put something of that persistence into Jacob himself.

JACOB IN THE END

We have a marvelous picture of Jacob in the end. He blessed and he worshiped, leaning on his staff. The natural strength of his self-life was broken. He had seen the face of the Lord. The last years of Jacob were filled with sorrow and beauty. First, he met himself in his twelve sons continually. He had a terrible time of it as he saw what he was in his own flesh and blood. He learned more and more deeply that only being transformed by the renewing of his mind could ever really do anything. But the most wonderful thing about this man was that he became a prince with God, and not only a prince with God, but a person who could impart blessings. Are you a person like that? When you meet others, do they get a blessing? I know people that do not have to open their mouths; you get a blessing by just being with them.

Jacob was also a worshiper. All God's overcomers are worshipers. What a change had come into this man. It was no longer what he got, but what he gave; no longer his satisfaction, but God's satisfaction. If the sun rose in Jacob's life on a twister, a swindler, a cheater, it set on a worshiper. The Bible, summing up the whole of that man's life, forgets and covers all the cheating, all the bargaining and says, "By faith, Jacob blessed the two sons of Joseph and worshiped, leaning on the top of his staff."

It is the most wonderful little phrase therefore that we find in Isaiah 33:23: "The lame took the prey." *That* is an overcomer. *That* is what it means to reign with Christ. Being crippled was the price, the cost, but through being crippled by the Lord, he became an overcomer, he gained the victory, he took the prey.

The other wonderful thing to any who know their Jacob-like nature is the fact that forever afterwards God calls Himself, not the God of Israel (now and again He calls Himself that), but He calls Himself hundreds and hundreds of times, the God of Jacob. This is an encouragement to every single child of God here and all through time, that God can bring a person like Jacob to the place of spiritual nobility, spiritual royalty.

The Lord of hosts is with us;
The God of Jacob is our refuge.
(Psalm 46:7 and 11)

OVERCOMING TO COME TO THE THRONE

Joseph

In this matter of reigning with Christ, Abraham, Isaac, and Jacob each illustrate one particular aspect of overcoming. Now let us consider Joseph, who draws the three together and binds the whole up into one. He is the end of a movement; the next movement is with Moses and Joshua. Joseph is a picture of an overcomer in a unique way. He is the normal picture, the picture that most people take as illustrating an overcomer. There are two scriptures in the New Testament that sum up the lesson of the life of Joseph:

> *And raised us up with him, and made us to sit with him in the heavenly places, in Christ Jesus. (Ephesians 2:6)*

> *If we endure, we shall also reign with him. (II Timothy 2:12)*

The old version says, *"If we suffer, we shall also reign with Him."* Really, when you look at Joseph, he is a remarkable person. Psalm 105 is a prophetic Psalm explaining his life to us:

> *And he called for a famine upon the land;*
> *He brake the whole staff of bread.*
> *He sent a man before them;*
> *Joseph was sold for a servant;*
> *His feet they hurt with fetters:*
> *He was laid in chains of iron,*
> *Until the time that his word came to pass,*
> *The word of the Lord tried him.*
> *The king sent and loosed him;*
> *Even the ruler of peoples, and let him go free.*
> *He made him lord of his house,*
> *And ruler of all his substance;*
> *To bind his princes at his pleasure,*
> *And teach his elders wisdom.*
> *Israel also came into Egypt.*

And Jacob sojourned in the land of Ham. (Psalm 105:16-23)

What an amazing prophetic insight into the whole story of Jacob! The Psalmist is saying that God sent a famine and broke the whole staff, man's natural sufficiency; then He sent a man before them. That man was Joseph. The remarkable thing was that he made that man go down and down and down before he went up and up and up. Before he came to the Pharaoh's throne and became *the* supreme power in Egypt, he had to go right down into Pharaoh's dungeon and stay there, seemingly rotting, unheard of, forgotten. Listen again to the prophecy over him by his beloved father, Jacob, in Genesis 49:22:

Joseph is a fruitful bough.
A fruitful bough by a fountain:
His branches run over the wall.

Do you get the picture? Here is a fountain and here is a tree. It has fruitful boughs for those within the wall, but his branches go over the wall to those who are without. What a picture of Joseph! He not only had something for the people of God, he had something for the unsaved. The whole of Egypt was saved and delivered through Joseph. *That* is overcoming. That is what it is to reign with Christ.

DIVINE REVELATION

We have the revelation of divine purpose concerning Joseph in Genesis 37:5-11. He was only a boy of sixteen or seventeen, and he had these magnificent dreams of sheaves of corn. All his brothers' sheaves bowed down before his, as did those of his mother and father. Then he saw the sun and the moon and the stars, and they all came and bowed to him. Do you mean to tell me your father and mother will come and bow to you and do obeisance?

Never scoff at someone to whom God gives a vision or a dream. (I do not mean some of those fraudulent things that now and again one hears about that are so way out that one feels ill.) Some people throw the baby out with the bath water and when someone has really seen something from the Lord, they tend to say, "Oh, I do not know."

If Joseph had come to me in this company, a boy of sixteen, and said, "I had a dream and in my dream I saw all of you bowing down," I would have said to the other brothers, "I think we had better pray for him." But you cannot just say, that there is nothing in it.

Why did the Lord give Joseph the dream? Later on, the Psalmist said, "Until the time came, the Word of the Lord tried him." That dream was the Word of the Lord, and in the end, when Joseph had been shaved of all his pride and self-sufficiency, it became a tremendous comfort to him that there was going to come a day when that dream would be fulfilled. Of course, when he was young he did not quite look at it like that, but it was divine revelation. Actually, God had unveiled his future. Who would have believed that young man, the youngest, save one, in the whole family, would one day be the supreme ruler of the greatest, most populous nation in the whole of the Middle East, and that he would become the means of salvation and deliverance for the whole family of Jacob? This purpose of God to bring Joseph to the throne and make him fruitful to all, could not be fulfilled through fleshly methods and fleshly means.

Now our way is this: if this is God's purpose, we want to get the man into a college of some kind, put him through the course, train him in a few public functions, give him public speaking and a few other things. We would not get him knocked about by his brothers and the Midianites. We would not sell him as a slave into an Egyptian household where by sheer faithfulness to God he overcame, even though he did not perhaps feel the need to be so faithful. After all, he was many, many miles from home and there was nothing to be lost by being unfaithful. Possibly, he had everything to gain by being unfaithful, since it was his master's wife. We would not think to put the boy into prison and leave him rotting there. You see, this is our whole problem in the matter of overcoming. Our ways and our methods are the ways of this world. Joseph could not come to such a place of reigning without much suffering and much discipline. His father said, "Joseph is a fruitful bough by a fountain of water whose boughs run over the wall." That was absolutely right. How did he become fruitful?

FELLOWSHIP OF HIS SUFFERINGS

He sent a man before them;
Joseph was sold for a servant:
His feet they hurt with fetters:
He was laid in chains of iron.
Until the time that his word came to pass,
The word of the Lord tried him. (Psalm 105:17-19)

That is suffering. In the Hebrew it is, "His soul entered into iron." Then I think of that verse in Philippians:

That I may know him, and the power of his resurrection, and the fellowship of his sufferings, becoming conformed unto his death. (Philippians 3:10)

Dear child of God, there is no way to come to kingship, there is no way to come to the throne, there is no way to reign with Christ, there is no overcoming without knowing the fellowship of His sufferings. I know of no other way.

Through many tribulations we must enter into the kingdom of God. (Acts 14:22)

We enter the kingdom of God by the salvation of God, by being born of God. That is not tribulation. However, to enter into kingship, to know something of reigning with Christ, to know the producing of a character, of spiritual capacity, *that* requires suffering and discipline.

And by reason of the exceeding greatness of the revelations, that I should not be exalted overmuch, there was given to me a thorn in the flesh, a messenger of Satan to buffet me, that I should not be exalted overmuch. Concerning this thing I besought the Lord thrice, that it might depart from me. And he hath said unto me, My grace is sufficient for thee: for my power is made perfect

*in weakness. Most gladly therefore will I rather glory in
my weaknesses, that the power of Christ may rest upon
me. (II Corinthians 12:7-9)*

It seems to me that whenever God gives revelation, He
gives a cross. I do not know of anyone in the ministry of God,
who has a real understanding of the things of God, without
some inexplicable cross. It is a principle with God. We see it
again, *par excellence,* in the apostle Paul. The higher he went,
and the deeper he saw into the purpose of God, into the heart
of God, the more God allowed this thorn in the flesh to keep
him humble. This is the thing we do not like. That is what
makes me sometimes suspicious in meetings where there
seems to be real vision and understanding with everyone getting so excited, yet there does not seem to be any thorn in the
flesh.

Who would have ever thought that God would give a
messenger of Satan? What do you think Potiphar was to
Joseph? What do you think his ten brothers were to him?
What do you think the Midianites were to him? Joseph was
marvelously brought up as a boy, but he was spoiled and his
father's darling. Then to be so ill-treated must have been to
him like a messenger of Satan because God had revealed
something to him. Remember that the next time you ask to
see something. God knows what He is doing with us.

*But we have this treasure in earthen vessels, that the
exceeding greatness of the power may be of God, and
not from ourselves; we are pressed on every side, yet not
straitened; perplexed, yet not unto despair; pursued, yet
not forsaken; smitten down, yet not destroyed; always
bearing about in the body the dying of Jesus, that the
life also of Jesus may be manifested in our body. For
we who live are always delivered unto death for Jesus'
sake, that the life also of Jesus may be manifested in
our mortal flesh. So then death worketh in us, but life
in you. (II Corinthians 4:7-12)*

That is the overcomer. *"Death worketh in us, but life in
you."* That is the principle. We must suffer; you get the joy.
But it is not that kind of suffering where it is apparent that you

are suffering for the Lord: "Oh, it is so hard to go on with the Lord. I have things that are coming my way that are hard and tough." No, the person who really suffers for the Lord knows what the Psalmist is saying, *"Who is the help of my countenance, and my God" (Psalm 42:11).* It is not leaving your face sallow and unwashed so that everyone knows you have been fasting. You give it a good scrub, clean it up, and look shining. No one smells any burning or singeing on you. They do not know. But it is death in you and life in them. That is the principle. After all, if someone were to say to you, "What about the future?" and you say, "perplexed." Perplexed? We send people to Bible college so they won't be perplexed. We do not expect people to go through theological training and all the rest of it to come out and be perplexed. They should have answers. That is why we send them there. That is what we pay them for. We do not expect anyone to be perplexed. This kind of testimony, "pressed on every side, perplexed, pursued, smitten down," does not seem much of a testimony. Remember, there is another side to it: life in them, death in us.

That is the whole principle that we have here in Joseph. It is the materials of the city, gold, precious stone and pearl. Every one of them come through suffering. Gold is refined until it is transparent as crystal. You have never seen such gold in your life. You can see right through it. That means it has been refined in a way that no gold has ever been refined on this earth. That is a picture of the fellowship of His sufferings; that is discipline. Precious stone is produced in the dark places of the earth by tremendous heat and pressure.

Pearls are produced in oysters. A little bit of grit gets on the softest part of the oyster. It tries to eject the grit by drawing out of the life within it some fluid which it wraps around the grit to make it less hurtful. The grit stays and the oyster goes through this process again and again. "My grace is sufficient for thee." And every time we prove His grace sufficient, another coat goes around the grit until a pearl is produced.

I wonder how many people get a bit of grit in their lives? They want to get rid of it so they go to the Lord and say, "Lord, this thing has got to go. It is destroying my home. It is destroying my Christian life. It is destroying my victory." They do not understand that God has allowed that thing in them. If they would only trust the Lord they would find there is a life in them, by the Spirit of God, which will put a coat around that bit of grit, and another and another. They may be a bit exhausted, but at the end they have a pearl. God has a pearl, and those pearls are the gates of the city through which people go in and out of the city, the place of judgment and counsel. Wisdom comes no other way. To come to the throne, we must not only know suffering, but we must know how to let go and how to humble ourselves.

> *But he that is greatest among you shall be your servant.*
> *And whosoever shall exalt himself shall be humbled;*
> *and whosoever shall humble himself shall be exalted.*
> *(Matthew 23:11-12)*

> *Humble yourselves in the sight of the Lord, and he*
> *shall exalt you. (James 4:10)*

> *Have this mind in you, which was also in Christ Jesus:*
> *who, existing in the form of God, counted not the being*
> *on an equality with God a thing to be grasped, but*
> *emptied himself, taking the form of a servant, being*
> *made in the likeness of men; and being found in fash-*
> *ion as a man, he humbled himself, becoming obedient*
> *even unto death, yea, the death of the cross. Wherefore*
> *also God highly exalted him, and gave unto him the*
> *name which is above every name; that in the name of*
> *Jesus every knee should bow, of things in heaven and*
> *things on earth and things under the earth, and that*
> *every tongue should confess that Jesus Christ is Lord,*
> *to the glory of God the Father. (Philippians 2:5-11)*

You have to go down to go up, but the world thinks that to go up you have got to go up. If you push others down on the way up, that has to be because that is the only way you can get up. Others have to be pushed aside in order for you to get up. That is *not* God's way. God's way to the throne is for you to go down, and the more you go down, the more you go up. Do not be afraid. The problem is not living, the problem is dying. Once we know how to die, once we know how to let go, once we know how to lose ourselves, we have the secret, for it is the infallible law of resurrection. The great key in Christian life, the great key in Christian service, the great key to church life is how to let go, how to fall into the ground, how to go down. Joseph had emphasized their bowing down to him in his dreams. He had said, "I saw you all bowing down, making obeisance to me." Experience made him their salvation and deliverance. One of the most beautiful chapters in Genesis says:

> *Then Joseph could not refrain himself before all them that stood by him; and he cried, Cause every man to go out from me. And there stood no man with him, while Joseph made himself known unto his brethren. And he wept aloud: and the Egyptians heard, and the house of Pharaoh heard. (Genesis 45:1-2)*

He did not say, "Now then, what about that dream? It has come to pass. Come on everybody, bow down. I have been waiting for this for years, you evil brothers. I am going to forgive you, but I am going to enjoy your bowing down." That is how we often feel. "I am going to forgive because one day, when I am there on the throne, I will not be bothered about little things like that, but I am going to enjoy being vindicated." But not Joseph. He does not want them to humble themselves. He says to them in the most beautiful words:

> *And now be not grieved, nor angry with yourselves, that ye sold me hither: for God did send me before you to preserve life. (Genesis 45:5)*

> *And God sent me before you to preserve you a remnant in the earth, and to save you alive by a great deliverance. So now it was not you that sent me hither, but God; and he hath made me a father to Pharaoh, and lord of all his house, and ruler over all the land of Egypt. (verses 7-8)*

That is overcoming. There is nothing elite about that, not elite in the sense that he is superior and thinks it. He is superior. He has something the other brothers do not have. He has a spiritual capacity that does not even want them to be angry with themselves nor to grieve for hours in repentance. He does not want them to grovel. He has come to the place now where all he wants is their blessing, their increase, their fruitfulness, their preservation, their deliverance, their glory. *That* is kingship, *that* is overcoming. That is the picture we see of our Lord Jesus who did exactly the same. He did not care for Himself. He did not preserve Himself. He did not try to win anything for Himself, not even the throne that was beyond His cross. It was all for us.

The brothers had terrible guilt complexes, as all do who ever do anything wrong to anybody, even when they have been forgiven. For years they go on thinking that person could never really forgive them. So when Jacob, their father, died, they thought Joseph would take the opportunity to get rid of them all. But he said:

> *Fear not; for am I in the place of God? And as for you, ye meant evil against me; but God meant it for good, to bring to pass, as it is this day, to save much people alive. (Genesis 50:19-20)*

We have the most wonderful picture of kingship here. There is no other way to the throne than this one of suffering and discipline. God does not want that faceless, characterless, bureaucracy that we know so much about in this world. He wants men and women conformed to His own image, to His own Son, who have been perfected through suffering. When a person has suffered, they are both firm and gentle. Any person who has suffered has compassion, but no compromise, and *that* is divine kingship. Oh, that God could teach us this lesson from the life of Joseph.

OVERCOMING TO POSSESS THE LAND

Moses

Exodus 15:2—The Lord is my strength and song, And he is become my salvation: This is my God, and I will praise him; My father's God, and I will exalt him.

Verses 13-14—Thou in thy lovingkindness hast led the people that thou hast redeemed: Thou hast guided them in thy strength to thy holy habitation. The peoples have heard, they tremble: Pangs have taken hold on the inhabitants of Philistia.

Verses 16-18—Terror and dread falleth upon them; By the greatness of thine arm they are as still as a stone; Till thy people pass over, O Lord, Till the people pass over that thou hast purchased. Thou wilt bring them in, and plant them in the mountain of thine inheritance, The place, O Lord, which thou hast made for thee to dwell in, The sanctuary, O Lord, which thy hands have established. The Lord shall reign for ever and ever.

We have seen represented in the lives of Abraham, Isaac, Jacob and Joseph one phase of God's dealing in this matter of kingship or reigning with Christ. Now, as we look at these verses, they sum up another phase of God's dealings as represented in the lives of Moses and Joshua. First, delivered, redeemed, saved, and then brought in and planted in the place which "Thou hast made for Thee to dwell in; Thy sanctuary O Lord." Oh, what a wonderful thing it is to know the object of our salvation!

It is interesting that in this song of Moses he speaks of the Passover not just being a getting out of Egypt, but a getting into the land. He speaks not merely about being delivered from the Egyptians, but being brought right through the wilderness and planted in the land, inheriting, coming to the place, the sanctuary of the Lord. The two-fold lesson we need to get hold of and understand in this matter of kingship is exactly what it is that God has done with us, and what is His objective in doing it.

Moses, in Hebrew, means "drawn out." Some people have said that it is an old Egyptian name which means "son", but it is much more likely that it just means "drawn out." You know if you are a child of God, that is written into your birthright; you have been drawn out. The wonderful thing is this, he was drawn out of water. Dear Moses had his own little exodus, only he was in a little bulrush, an ark, as it were. He had his own exodus; it was in him. Before ever he could be used to lead the people of God through the Red Sea, he had an experience of God that was written right into his very being. That is one of the great lessons of kingship. You and I can never lead the people of God into anything until God does it first in us. We have to know something of the sovereignty of the Lord, the provision of the Lord, the deliverance of the Lord, the liberating power of the Lord if we are to bring others out, to see others delivered, to see others saved, to see others freed. It is all a part of this matter of redemption.

What is the lesson of Moses' life? In actual fact you will see all the way through Moses' life an identification with his experience and the people's experience. There is no doubt to me that Moses' whole life was determined by that tremendous encounter with the Lord when he was about eighty years of age.

> *And the angel of the Lord appeared unto him in a flame of fire out of the midst of a bush: and he looked, and behold, the bush burned with fire, and the bush was not consumed. And Moses said, I will turn aside now, and see this great sight, why the bush is not burnt. And when the Lord saw that he turned aside to see, God called unto him out of the midst of the bush, and said, Moses, Moses. And he said, Here am I. And he said, Draw not nigh hither: put off thy shoes from off thy feet, for the place whereon thou standest is holy ground. Moreover he said, I am the God of thy father, the God of Abraham, the God of Isaac, and the God of Jacob. And Moses hid his face; for he was afraid to look upon God. (Exodus 3:2-6)*

And Moses said unto God, Behold, when I come unto the children of Israel, and shall say unto them, The God of your fathers hath sent me unto you; and they shall say to me, What is his name? what shall I say unto them? And God said unto Moses, I AM THAT I AM: and he said, Thus shalt thou say unto the children of Israel, I AM hath sent me unto you. (verses 13-14)

In this encounter of God with Moses, we have one of the greatest lessons in kingship that it is possible to learn. For really, that thorn bush was Moses and the flame of fire was God. What God was saying in effect to Moses was this: Until you, a dried-up, dead, old thorn bush, and I, the eternal fire, get together nothing will be done. But once I get into you and become the flame of eternal fire in you, you become eternal fuel for eternal fire. Then the purpose of God for the nation and for the nations will be fulfilled. It is a lesson we find very, very hard to learn. You do not normally go to a Bible college to get turned out a dried-up, old thorn bush. You do not go to a theological seminary to be turned out a dried-up, old thorn bush. You do not start studying the Bible to become a dried-up, old thorn bush. It is a very hard lesson for us to learn.

It took the Lord forty years to get Moses from thinking that he was some magnificent, stately palm tree to recognizing himself as a dried-up, dead, old thorn bush, two-a-penny in the desert. Years ago, I used to wonder why the Lord did not appear in another way. Wouldn't it have been marvelous if it had been a stately palm tree? After all, there are quite a few palm trees in the Sinai wilderness. If there had been one of those magnificent, palm trees with its great fronds out in a blaze of fire when Moses came near, immediately he would have gone because it would have been an unusual sight to see a palm tree on fire. Then God would have said majestically, as He looked down at Moses, "Do not come any nearer; the ground you are standing on is holy."

Everyone who knows anything about their Bible would be thrilled with the biblical typology because the palm tree is a symbol of righteousness and holiness and fruitfulness. Oh, how wonderful; holy, holy, holy is the Lord God, the Almighty. Then they would have linked it with the law of God, the holiness of God, the truth of God, the righteousness of God, and the glory of God. It would have been absolutely marvelous, but the Lord did not do it.

Why didn't God choose the acacia tree? The acacia tree (shittim tree in the Authorized Version) is perhaps the most beautiful of the trees in the desert. It is delicate and very beautiful. I suppose it is the only real tree you have in the southern part of the wilderness of Sinai. If God had appeared in the shittim tree in a blaze of fire and the tree had not been consumed, we Bible students would have had a wonderful time thinking God was saying, "Moses, this is the tree out of which all the furniture of My dwelling place is going to be made. I am the fire and this is you." But God did not choose the shittim tree.

Or we might have thought the Lord would have chosen a vine or an olive tree with all their spiritual significance and symbolism, although they do not exist in that part of the desert. No, God chose the commonest, ugliest, most worthless of all the vegetation of the desert. Even a camel, if it can find something else to eat, will turn up its nose at a thorn bush. Yet God chose the thorn bush and got into it. Now I have never seen a thorn bush taller than myself, and even when you see such a big one, it is really quite magnificent. Most of them are really scrubby little things. Can't you see how amazing it was? There, close to the desert ground in a thorn bush that was no longer green or flowering, but one that had lived its life and died, its resources drained, its energy finished, dried-up and dead, God entered into it. Later Moses said, "The grace of Him that dwelleth in the bush." He never called it a tree; he called it a bush. And God spoke up at Moses and said, "Moses, Moses."

When Moses first saw that bush on fire, he undoubtedly thought, "Oh, this is just another thorn bush on fire that the sun has ignited." And he went on keeping his sheep. About ten minutes later when he turned around and saw it, he may have thought, "Now that is some thorn bush," and went on looking after the sheep. But half an hour later he thought, "I must turn aside to see this great sight. This is the biggest thorn bush in the whole desert." Then God spoke, not from above the thorn bush, not from around the thorn bush, but out of the midst of a common, ugly, worthless, dead, thorn bush.

What was God saying? God was saying, "Moses, you thought that because you were brought up in the world as the son of Pharaoh's daughter that you were a palm tree. You are not. When I first got you out into this desert you thought you were the shittim tree, an acacia tree, something I could use, but you are not. Before ever I can make you a palm tree, before ever I can make you the acacia tree, you must first learn that you are a thorn bush." That, I say, is the hardest lesson for believers to learn. Anyone who is coming to the throne has got to learn that they are nothing more than a dried-up, old, thorn bush, two-a-penny.

Perhaps, in some glorious convention, you said you wanted to reign with Christ. Some great word came about exercising authority in the name of the Lord and you got so thrilled and challenged by it that when the appeal was given you stood up and said, "Yes, Lord, I want to exercise authority in Thy name." Ever since then everything has gone wrong. You thought you were a palm tree, "Ah yes, now is a new day for me; I stood up. The new day begins."

It certainly was, only not quite the new day you thought. What God began to do was say, "Yes, but before ever you can reign with Me, before ever you can exercise authority, you have got to come to the place where you know what you are naturally." But that is only the first lesson. God help us if we stay with what we are naturally. The second lesson is the flame of fire. Then we know that God is the flame of fire, He is the glory, He is the power, He is the life, He is the light, He is everything. The third lesson is that the dried-up, worthless, thorn bush and the flame of fire have got to get together. The amazing thing is that the thorn bush remains the thorn bush, and the fire remains the fire. That is really the lesson of kingship. **You will never have it in yourself; it is always the Lord in you.**

I AM THAT I AM

I remember, years ago, puzzling and puzzling and puzzling over this unmentionable name of God. I was never satisfied with those wonderful thoughts that were passed on to us by various preachers about the infinity of God, the fact that God has no beginning and no end, that He is everywhere at the same time, that He knows everything. They said that is what I AM THAT I AM means. He has no beginning, He had no end, He is all powerful, almighty, He is everywhere at the same time, everything consists by Him. But somehow it never satisfied me.

One day a little old Irish evangelist came to this place. He was not so highly educated, but oh what a lovely, dear brother he was. He preached one Sunday morning on I AM THAT I AM, and he just said one thing that unlocked the whole matter for me. He said, "You know, I think God was giving Moses a blank check. I AM. . . add what you need. Do you need love? I AM love. Do you need power? I AM power. Do you need grace? I AM grace. Do you need life? I AM life. Do you need light? I AM the light of the world."

Then everything fell into place. Jesus said, "I AM the bread of life." Jesus said, "I AM the light of the world." Jesus said, "Before Abraham was, I AM." John later wrote, "God IS light. God IS love." Suddenly, the whole thing fell into place. We are the thorn bush, God is the I AM in us, and everything we need we can add to the I AM. What a name!

Of course, God has no beginning and no end. Of course, God is everywhere at the same time. Of course, God knows everything, but that does not necessarily help me; I know nothing. I cannot be everywhere at the same time. I am a little, finite, created bit of clay, tied to one place. Sometimes I wish I had a hundred bodies to run around with, but then I would get into a greater mess than I am. God's majesty and His infinity cause me to bow before Him and worship Him. That I recognize absolutely, but it does not meet my need. However, I find that the I AM THAT I AM has vouchsafed to me everything that He is. He says, "I will get into you; I will breathe through you; I will love through you; I will speak through you; I will work through you. I will be everything in you if only you will be a thorn bush, if only you will recognize that you are not even a living thorn bush, but you are a dried-up, dead, old thorn bush. Let Me get in you and I will do the work. The two of us together, the flame of fire and the thorn bush, will see the purpose of God fulfilled, will see nations touched, will see My will done on earth as it is in heaven, will see My kingdom coming." It is a great lesson—kingship.

Of course, Israel had to learn it, too. Moses' name means *drawn out*. Israel was drawn out. They also knew what it was to be drawn out of Egypt, redeemed with so great a redemption. The wonderful thing about being drawn out of Egypt was that God immediately began to teach them what He had taught Moses. They could not get across that Red Sea. God had to do it. Moses stood there with a little rod that he lifted up. He spoke a few words and the east wind blew, the sea was piled up, and they went across as on dry ground. Their deliverance became the destruction of the Egyptian host.

God began to teach those people they could not save themselves. No sooner had they eaten the Passover lamb and the Angel of Death passed over them than they had their first big problem. They could not get across the sea. Only the Lord could do it. But no sooner were they on the other side, than they had the next great problem. They had no water. They came to a place where the water was brackish and they could not drink it because it would only make them more thirsty than ever. They began to grumble and moan, and then a tree was thrown in and it became sweet water. It was the Lord, Christ crucified. Later on, it was water out of the rock, Christ crucified. There was manna miraculously provided six days out of seven and on the sixth day, two portions. Then it was a pillar of cloud and fire.

Have you ever heard of anything like it? They had no committees, no councils, no great sessions saying, "Oh, shall we go this way? Shall we go that way? Shall we do this? What do you think? So-and-so thinks this; so-and-so thinks that. So-and-so thinks from this past history we should do this." No, the Lord was their guidance. As soon as they saw Him moving, they packed up their tents and were on the move. The Lord was everything. What He taught Moses, He now taught them all the way through the forty years in the wilderness. This matter of kingship is a wonderful lesson as we see it in the life of Moses.

Yet now, if thou wilt forgive their sin—; and if not, blot me, I pray thee, out of thy book which thou hast written. (Exodus 32:32)

This was not the old Moses. This was a new Moses in whom the Lord was everything. The Spirit of Christ in him exhibited the very same nature that later the Lord Jesus was to express when He laid down His life for us all. That is kingship. There was no self-glory, no self-ambition, no self-interest, no pomp and show. There was no, "I am here. I have this title, I have this status, I have this background." No, it was true service. This kind of king exists for the people.

JOSHUA

When we come to Joshua, we have the second part of the story. In the Greek, Joshua is *Jesus*. It is the Old Testament form of Jesus, *the Lord is salvation*. The wonderful thing about Joshua is that he illustrates the other side of the coin. Have you learned that the Lord is your salvation? It is not only that He gives salvation, not only that He saves, but *He is your salvation.* You have learned that you are nothing and that God is everything and that it is the two of you together. Now you must go in and get it. That is the great lesson of Joshua. You must go over and possess your possessions; you must inherit your inheritance. You must go in by faith, using the soles of your feet, and take what is yours. Dear child of God, all this business about whether there is a second experience, or a second blessing, or a baptism of the Spirit is solved, in my estimation, in this one simple thing. The Lord has given you everything, but unless you go in and possess it, you will not experience it.

POSSESSING THE POSSESSION

Every place that the sole of your foot shall tread upon, to you have I given it, as I spake unto Moses. From the wilderness, and this Lebanon, even unto the great river, the river Euphrates, all the land of the Hittites, and unto the great sea toward the going down of the sun, shall be your border. (Joshua 1:3-4)

It is the soles of your feet that matter. There are people who say, "Thank God, all I am is an old, dried-up thorn bush and yes, the Lord is everything." But really, they do not have much. We wonder why they always say they have everything when they are so dreary. There are people who say, "I have everything in the Lord. I do not need any more." But they are so dreary. Their lives are so colorless, so drab, so unoriginal. You do not touch the Lord in them. What is wrong? I am not asking for just emotion and excitement and all that kind of thing, but it is not good enough to learn the lesson that the Lord is everything and that you are nothing. Now the Lord in you has got to go forward and you have got to put the sole of your foot down. Isn't it interesting that the time before it was a little rod. This time it was feet, and feet had to get wet.

My dear friend, have you got your feet wet yet? Some people have gone over the Red Sea but they have not gotten their feet wet in the Jordan. Until you put the soles of your feet down, the water will never pile up at Adam. That which God has done in Christ in crucifying your old man, in putting away the old man, in abolishing the old Adam, cannot be made real in your life until you put your feet down. You cannot know the ark of the covenant and all its glory and power, you cannot know the walls of Jericho coming down, you cannot know what it is to say with Joshua, "Give me this mountain," until you put your feet down.

Through Faith and Patience

That ye be not sluggish, but imitators of them who through faith and patience inherit the promises. (Hebrew 6:12)

At the beginning when they put their feet down in the river Jordan, they did not need too much patience because the moment the soles of their feet went down onto the river bed, water piled up at Adam, and they went over. But they needed a bit of patience when they came to Jericho. Can't you just hear the legalists? "Look here Joshua, you have got this whole thing wrong. You are going back on the Lord. The Lord said that every place the sole of your foot treads upon He will give you. All we had to do was put the soles of our feet down and the water was immediately cut off. Now what is all this about going around once a day for six days and seven times on the seventh day in the heat of Jericho? You must be crazy. It is the lowest place on the earth. How awful to go round and round Jericho. Once a day for six days is bad enough, but seven times on the seventh day! I think this is just unbelief. We could get this thing settled in an instant if we had enough faith. Blow the trumpets, put our feet down; blow the trumpets and see the wall come down."

But there are times when it takes a good deal more than putting the sole of your feet down once to see the Lord act. You have to have faith and patience and then you inherit the promise.

What does Joshua teach us? Joshua just teaches us this one simple lesson: once we know what it is to be saved, once we have begun to learn the lesson that we are nothing and God is everything and it is a union between God and us, (that is the key to it all) *then* we must go over the Jordan and possess the promises of God. We shall never see the house of God built in the desert. We shall never see the purpose of God fulfilled in forty years of going round. But isn't it true, that much of our church life is just an endless going round the wilderness, not for forty years but four hundred? We go round and round and round, always knowing the Lord but never possessing. Isn't it true of your life and my life? Many of us are ever learning and never coming to a knowledge of the truth. We learn and we learn and we learn, but we never possess. Our great need, as we see from the life of Joshua, is that if we are going to come to the throne, we have to learn to possess and we do it with the soles of our feet, figuratively speaking.

Another Spirit

Another thing I would like to mention in the life of Joshua is that Joshua and Caleb possessed the land because they were of another Spirit. You and I could ponder on that for a long, long time. The key to possessing our inheritance is the gracious ministry of the Holy Spirit, Captain of the Lord's host, Angel of His presence. Oh, dear child of God, do not be afraid of the Person of the Holy Spirit. Do not be put off by what is excessive, extreme or false. On the other hand, do not just feel that the Holy Spirit is some agent. It is amazing to me how the people of God give a place to the Father and a place to the Son and hardly any place to the Holy Spirit. It is as if the Spirit of God is some impersonal agent that just does things almost without being a person. But, it is the Person of the Father, and the Person of the Lord Jesus, and the Person of the Holy Spirit. You grieve the Holy Spirit when you treat Him as a thing, as an it. No one can have real faith without the Spirit of God.

When those spies went into the land, ten of them that came back had no faith. They said, "We cannot do it. It is a beautiful land flowing with milk and honey, but it is fortified to the heavens and the people are like giants. We cannot do it."

Two of them, Joshua and Caleb, said, "We are well able; for if the Lord is with us, we shall inherit." They were of another Spirit.

Hidden Sin

The other thing about this matter of Joshua is an uncomfortable one, and that is Achan. Where there is sin there will be a paralyzing of any inheritance, and you cannot bury it. Achan stole things, poor man, and then he buried them in his tent. Isn't it silly? Isn't sin a stupidity? He took those beautiful Babylonian garments and he could not wear them; he could not sell them. He took the shekels of gold and silver and he could never do anything with them. Many of us do that kind of thing. We fall into sin and then we bury it. There is no satisfaction, there is no fulfillment. There is only an awful sense of living a facade, of being a hypocrite. Do not think because you have buried it out of your sight, it is out of the sight of God. He sees what is buried in every home. You may have buried it, but God sees it, and sooner or later your whole life will hinge upon that matter being settled. So it was with Achan. And that is why one of the prophets calls the valley of Achor a door of hope.

Thank God, there is someone else who was stoned to death for us, but the principle is still the same. If we have sinned or fallen into sin and there is something buried in our lives or in our family circumstances, until it comes out into the light and is judged and put away by the finished work of

Christ, by the blood of the Lamb, it will effectively stop you from entering in **and** will stop the people of God from entering in. The Lord Jesus has vested in you and in me the kingship which His Father vested in Him.

> *He that overcometh, I will give to him to sit down with me in my throne, as I also overcame, and sat down with my Father in his throne. (Revelation 3:21)*

I am quite sure that there is so much for us to possess. There is a fulness in Christ for many of us to possess. There is an anointing of the Holy Spirit that many of us need to possess. There is a ministry, whatever it is, that we need to possess. There is a functioning in the body of Christ which we need to possess. There are enemies we need to see destroyed, putting our feet down upon their neck. There are areas that need to be brought under the domain of the authority of the Lord Jesus Christ—things personal, things family, things to do with us locally, things to do with the people of God nationally and in the whole world. Oh, if God could bring us to the place where we know something of reigning with Christ, it would be a new chapter. If we learn the lesson of Moses and the lesson of Joshua, we shall know something of entering in and possessing what the Lord has so dearly won for us. May the Lord help us.

REIGNING TO BUILD GOD'S HOUSE

David

Luke 22:29-30 (NEB) And now I vest in you the kingship which my Father vested in me; you shall eat and drink at my table in my kingdom and sit on thrones as judges of the twelve tribes of Israel.

I Chronicles 29:1-19

Here we have another phase in this whole matter of reigning with Christ and the principles of kingship; what the Bible calls *having dominion.* We have been looking at characteristics of kingship as we find them in some of the saints in the Old Testament. The first phase we saw was in the lives of Abraham, Isaac, Jacob, and Joseph. In many ways, in these four lives we see the essential, foundational elements in true kingship and overcoming. That is why God is ever after called the God of Abraham, Isaac, and Jacob.

Then we came to the second phase in God's dealings with His people which is summed up in the lives of those two great men, Moses and Joshua. That was all to do with possessing the land, or if you like it another way, redemption, being delivered from Egypt, in order that we might pass over and enter into our inheritance. Or to put it another way, it is all to do with appropriating our resources in Christ, with the fulness of God in Christ by the Holy Spirit. God has to be everything and we can be nothing. When we learn that lesson, that Christ is the I AM in us, then we are ready to go over and possess the land. Then we saw that it is only what we put the soles of our feet upon that we get. We get nothing more and nothing less than what we put the soles of our feet upon. So that is the great lesson of Moses and Joshua.

Now we come to the third phase where this matter of kingship is more clearly defined than in any of the others, and we see something of the heart of God's purpose. It is worthy of note that the Spirit of God first gives us a record of these events in I and II Samuel and I and II Kings. These four books in the Greek version of the Old Testament are called *The Four Books of the Kingdom.* In those four books the Holy

Spirit has recorded for us the whole history of the kings, the throne, and the coming in of the kingdom. He begins with Samuel, who is one of the great turning points of the Bible. Samuel was really the king maker. He was the one that God used to bring in the king, first the false king and then the true king. From then on, we have the whole history of the kings, the division later into Israel and Judah, and the false kingdom, not the Messianic line, not the royal line of David.

The Holy Spirit gives us the history of the king on the throne, the kingdom, how it came in, how we got the king of God's choice, God's watching over the throne, and the kingdom right the way through. Then, having given us the record or the history, He goes right back again, this time to Adam, and records the whole thing again in the Book of Chronicles. He goes swiftly at first from Adam over all those centuries to David. Then quite exhaustively, from David onwards, the Holy Spirit records the whole thing a second time. Now why?

It is always very interesting in the Bible whenever God says something twice. Deuteronomy is the giving of the law the second time. Chronicles is the giving of the history of God's dealings with man all over again. Why did God do it? It is because the Lord first speaks about the kingdom and the king and then about the house of God and worship. In I and II Samuel and I and II Kings, we have the history from the point of view of the kingdom and the throne. In Chronicles we have the whole history told to us again, only this time from the point of view of the house of God, worship, and the service of the house of God. These two matters are intimately linked together, and that is why we are going to look at them in the life of David and the life of Solomon. These two men are the beginning and the end of a matter, and they exemplify and illustrate for us the link between kingship and the house of God.

We must learn one simple lesson. If the house of God is to be built, we have got to reign with Christ *now*. If we are really going to obey that injunction of the apostle Paul by the Spirit of God, "Let all things be done unto building up," we must learn to reign. The one thing the enemy will do is see to it that we do not build one another up. He will make sure that every contribution we make is superficial or spurious, that it is just wood, hay and stubble, that it does not have the character of Christ in it. He will do everything to fill our times with hot air or with natural activity and routine, just the things that anyone can do. That is why it is so important that everyone of us who are members of the body of Christ, who are living stones quarried out of the very life of God Himself, in Christ, should learn to reign in the *now*.

That is why, once we see this matter, God allows all kinds of things to come into our lives, often inexplicable things. It is because we have got to learn to come up. God allows us to go down in order that we can learn how to come up. We have to learn the principle that before you can come up, you must go down. It is the exact opposite of this world's way of looking at things: everything that goes up, comes down. But God's law is that everything that goes down, comes up. If you humble yourself, you will be exalted; if you fall into the ground and die there will be a harvest; if you are prepared to humble yourself to the death of the cross, God will exalt you to the throne of God.

And I also say unto thee, that thou art Peter, and upon this rock I will build my church; and the gates of Hades shall not prevail against it. I will give unto thee the keys of the kingdom of heaven: and whatsoever thou shalt bind on earth shall be bound in heaven; and whatsoever thou shalt loose on earth shall be loosed in heaven. (Matthew 16:18-19)

We see here that there is a connection between gates of hell prevailing or not prevailing against the building work of Christ with the keys of the kingdom of heaven. In other words, if you and I do not learn to reign with Christ, to exercise the authority that we have in the name of Jesus Christ, if we do not learn to use the keys of the kingdom of heaven, then the gates of hell will prevail against the building work of Christ.

You see, the whole problem is this. If we take the words of our Lord Jesus Christ, how can we explain church history? We have to say when we look at it with a candid, open-hearted, sincere mind, that again and again and again the gates of hell have prevailed. It is all very well to take that adage that is so common in evangelical circles that it is all invisible. But it seems to me a strange way to get out of it. If it is all invisible, we never sense it, we never touch it, we never see it, we apparently never get involved in it. Things can be hopelessly fragmented down here, in awful error and darkness and decline, and somehow or other, all that wonderful work is yet being done in the unseen. I cannot believe it. I am quite sure that the essential work of building the church *is* invisible. However, it must have a *visible* expression. Somewhere, somehow, through some saints, there must be a visible, concrete expression of the work of Christ. Is it possible that when a person is born again, I am not to see a single evidence of the work of Christ in their lives, nor see any fruit, that it is all invisible, that however they live, however they behave, whatever words they use, they are saved and they are growing in the Lord? Of course not! Our Lord said, "By their fruits ye shall know them." When a person is converted, it is a work of the Holy Spirit.

> *The wind bloweth where it will, and thou hearest the voice thereof, but knowest not whence it cometh, and whither it goeth: so is every one that is born of the Spirit. (John 3:8)*

We know that. Nevertheless, when a person is born of God, we see a new light in his eyes, we see a cleaning up of that outward person, we begin to see him coming under the discipline of the Spirit of God, we begin to see a change taking place in his life. The loose sin that he could indulge in before, he no longer can indulge in. We see him growing in the Lord. We see a hunger for prayer, a hunger for the things of God, a hunger for the Word of God. He begins to testify before others. Something is happening and we rejoice. We know that it is not just the outward techniques and methods that mean anything, but there is evidence that something which is essentially eternal and spiritual has taken place in this person's life and there is an outward expression. So it is with the church.

How then can we explain this word which is in many ways ambiguous? It can be translated two ways: "Upon this rock I will build my church, and the gates of hell shall not prevail against it." That is, when the gates of hell come against the building work of Christ, it shall not prevail. The power of the gates of hell will be broken and that building work of Christ will go on. Or it can be seen the other way: "Upon this rock I will build my church, and the gates of hell shall not hold out against it." In other words, there are times when the church that Christ is building barges in, as it were, and goes right into the very kingdom of the power of darkness and takes out lives in the name of the Lord Jesus Christ. There are lives that are bound and fettered in sin and moral and spiritual darkness. We can preach at them until we are blue in the face, but until someone can use the keys of the kingdom of heaven somewhere in the unseen, behind the scenes as it were, nothing happens.

It seems to me that in Scripture *gates* symbolize counsel. It is where the elders always sat giving judgment. In the old days, you could go to the elders sitting in the gate, and you could have your problems sorted out by them. They would arbitrate, adjudicate, give counsel, and give the ruling of the Word of God, the Law upon any matter. They sat in the gates, and therefore, the gates became a symbol of counsel, of purpose, of judgment.

Now the gates of hell surely mean that. The powers of darkness have a purpose, a counsel, a design. They have a plan. You and I, covered in our Lord, a life hid with Christ in God, under His headship, must learn to use the keys of the kingdom of heaven. In the New American Standard Bible this is put in a somewhat awkward way, but it is the most literally accurate way that it can be put in English:

> *And whatever you shall bind on earth shall have been bound in heaven, and whatever you shall loose on earth shall have been loosed in heaven. (Matthew 16:19b)*

It is not that we are saying, "We have decided this, Lord, fall in step. We have decided that this and this will take place and we want You to get behind us. We are using the keys." No. It is that, by the Spirit of God, we have sensed the will of God. We have come to know in our spirit together, what is the will of God in this particular thing we are facing. And we know that it is the will of God that these powers of darkness in this matter should be bound. That is what it means when it says of the Lord Jesus in that Messianic Psalm 110: "Rule thou in the midst of thine enemies."

We need to learn this simple lesson of kingship, of reigning with Christ now. We learn this lesson of overcoming in the lives of David and Solomon because, before the house of God could be built, David had to come to the throne. The wrong man on the throne had to be taken off and put away. The right man had to be drawn to the throne and placed on the throne. It was only when David became king and fought all the enemies of God's purpose and defeated them that his son, rightly named Solomon (*peace*), could take the throne. All this has tremendous lessons for us because overcoming has very much to do with the building of the house of God.

> *And I turned to see the voice that spake with me. And having turned I saw seven golden candlesticks; and in the midst of the candlesticks one like unto a son of man, clothed with a garment down to the foot, and girt about at the breasts with a golden girdle. (Revelation 1:12-13)*

> *The mystery of the seven stars which thou sawest in my right hand, and the seven golden candlesticks. The seven stars are the angels of the seven churches: and the seven candlesticks are seven churches. (verse 20)*

I recently saw an unfortunate tract which had an old oil lamp on one side and a few other things on the other that supposedly were all to do with the book of Revelation. This lampstand is not that, but is the seven-branch lampstand, the Menorah, of the tabernacle in the Old Testament. It has always been a symbol of divine light. When we come to the New Testament, that lampstand is a symbol of the testimony of Jesus.

> *And he said unto me, What seest thou? And I said, I have seen, and behold, a [lampstand] all of gold, with its bowl upon the top of it, and its seven lamps thereon; there are seven pipes to each of the lamps, which are upon the top thereof. (Zechariah 4:2)*

Then the angel that talked with me answered and said unto me, Knowest thou not what these are? And I said, No, my lord. Then he answered and spake unto me, saying, This is the word of the Lord unto Zerubbabel, saying, Not by might, nor by power, but by my Spirit, saith the Lord of hosts. Who art thou, O great mountain? before Zerubbabel thou shalt become a plain; and he shall bring forth the top stone with shoutings of Grace, grace, unto it. Moreover the word of the Lord came unto me, saying, The hands of Zerubbabel have laid the foundation of this house; his hands shall also finish it; and thou shalt know that the Lord of host hath sent me unto you. (verses 5-9)

This lampstand all of gold, is a symbol of a building program. The testimony of Jesus is that God had in His heart from the very beginning a building program. He wanted to make us human beings living stones to be built together into His own eternal habitation. He wanted a home for Himself in the Spirit, from which His light would shine forth, from which His love would be expressed, from which His life would be manifested. He wanted that home, that bride, that city, that temple of the Lord to be the place from which God would rule the whole universe. It is a most glorious purpose God has for us, that we, in union with Him, should have dominion.

It is interesting that when we come to the end of the Old Testament, we find a lampstand all of gold, and we hear the words, "Not by might, nor by power, but by My Spirit, saith the Lord of hosts." When we come to the end of the New Testament, we find seven golden lampstands, and in the midst of them, the risen Son of God speaking to each one. These lampstands represent building programs of seven local churches selected to represent the whole church of God in time and on earth. What does the Lord say to each one? "To him that overcomes . . . to him that overcomes . . . to him that overcomes." Then He says, "He that hath an ear to hear, let him hear what the Spirit says to the churches." *Not by might, nor by power, but by My Spirit, saith the Lord of hosts.* In other words, when we come to this whole matter of overcoming, it has a tremendous amount to do with the building of the house of God.

People always rush up to me after meetings and say, "What about those poor saints who are scattered out in rural areas who have absolutely no fellowship?" My dear friend, why not leave them to God? It is the same as the kind of question we are always hearing, "What about the unsaved who have never heard?" If you are so concerned about the unsaved who have never heard, don't you think God is? Do you think God is going to judge them just like that? Do you think God is less righteous than you? We try to take the whole matter of judgment out of the hands of God, and we do not really trust Him wholly on it. God will be neither sentimental nor severe; He will be true. All through the ages there have been people who have obeyed the light that God has given them, and in that sense, they are overcomers. All that is required of you is to obey implicitly, explicitly all that God has shown to you. Never deny it, never contradict it, and never compromise on it. Leave the dear ones who are out in rural areas and scattered parts of the earth where they have no fellowship to God, and think for a few moments of those of us who have every opportunity of fellowship.

My point is that overcoming is not just a matter to do with your personal life. It is true that our Lord said, "To him that overcometh", not "to those who overcometh." In that sense it is a personal matter, but it has very much to do with your relationship to other people of God. You cannot withdraw and live like a hermit. You cannot just say, "As long as I go on with the Lord personally, that is all that matters." No, it has much to do with this matter of the building of the house of God. So we see in the lives of David and Solomon the beginning and the end of a matter. In David we have the preparation for the building of the house, and vital principles are illustrated in his life. In Solomon we have the realization of that purpose to build that house.

PREPARATION FOR BUILDING THE HOUSE

But now thy kingdom shall not continue: The Lord hath sought him a man after his own heart, and the Lord hath appointed him to be prince over his people, because thou hast not kept that which the Lord commanded thee. (I Samuel 13:14)

*And when he had removed him, he raised up David to
be their king; to whom also he bare witness and said, I
have found David the son of Jesse, a man after my
[own] heart, who shall do all my will.* *(Acts 13:22)*

A Person After God's Own Heart

I wonder what it means, "after God's own heart." I feel
that it has something to do with those words of the Father
concerning our Lord when He went into the waters of Jordan
to be baptized. The heavens opened and the voice of God was
heard saying, "This is My beloved Son in whom I am well
pleased." What God was really saying was, "Like Father, like
Son. He is displaying the same heart quality and attitude as
My own."

Those waters of baptism were not that He might wash
away sins; He had no sins to wash away. They were not that
He might go through an empty ritual; God does not believe
just in that. Those waters of baptism for Jesus represented
Calvary three years before He came to it. They represented
the death of the cross, and it was as if God were saying, "Will
you or won't you? You do not have to. Will you or will you
not?" And Jesus stepped down into those waters and committed Himself to the death of the cross. When that happened
the heavens opened, the Spirit of God came down and
anointed Him, and the voice of God said, "Like Father, like
Son."

It happened again on the Mount of Transfiguration.
Jesus turned away from His glory and went down to face the
epileptic, demon-possessed boy. It was only just a few weeks
from His cross. He could have stepped into glory at that
point, but He turned away. Then God said, "This is My Son,
hear ye Him." It is a matter of character, a man after God's
own heart.

In I Samuel 9:2, we are told that Saul was head and
shoulders above all the people and was goodly to look at and
strong. He was everything that anyone would have ever
thought should be a king. He had the bearing, the physique,
the looks, the strength, and the personality evidently. He had
all the outward characteristics of a king, but compare that with
I Samuel 16:6,7,13. There, Samuel saw the first of Jesse's sons

and said, "This must be he," but the Lord told him not to look at the appearance, but look on the heart. Dear Samuel received a check in his spirit, and he looked at seven of Jesse's sons and said, "No." The last one was not there because they had not even bothered to bring David in. (Jewish tradition tells us that David was very much younger than his youngest brother.)

Then Samuel said, "Is there another?"

And Jesse said, "Yes, there is another, but you do not want to see him, do you? He is out with the sheep."

And Samuel said, "Yes, I want to see him." As soon as he saw him he said, "Yes."

David was of a ruddy complexion, a good countenance, and was all beautiful, which means he was quite nice to look at. But you see, he was too young. The point was that apparently he was not God's man because he was too young.

As the youngest of all the brothers, David must have had some tough times out there with the sheep. Mind you, some youngest children are pretty resilient. They sort of make up for the fact that they are the youngest. It is quite wrong to think that the youngest do not have the most character and will not go the farthest because John Wesley was the twenty-second and Charles Wesley was the twenty-third. So we have examples in Scripture of the first-born being everything and we also have examples of the last-born being everything.

David was the youngest, and outwardly he did not appear to be the man of God's choice. We know by what we have been told of David's life that he had a number of experiences, and in those experiences he proved the Lord. That is how you become a man or a woman after God's own heart. It is not in the great, open, public arena. It is so often in your routine job, or in your home, or in your relationship with parents or with others that you are put to the test. It is there that your heart attitude is revealed.

Clear-sighted Understanding

Would to God that every Christian had as clear an understanding of God's purpose as David did. His reigning, his throne, and his kingdom were not just something in his mind, but they were a responsibility to discharge, a responsibility to fulfill God's purpose.

And it came to pass, when David dwelt in his house, that David said to Nathan the prophet, Lo, I dwell in a house of cedar, but the ark of the covenant of the Lord dwelleth under curtains. And Nathan said unto David, Do all that is in thy heart; for God is with thee. And it came to pass the same night, that the word of God came to Nathan, saying, Go and tell David my servant, Thus saith the Lord, Thou shalt not build me a house to dwell in. (I Chronicles 17:1-4)

[Solomon] shall build me a house, and I will establish his throne for ever. I will be his father, and he shall be my son: and I will not take my lovingkindness away from him, as I took it from him that was before thee; but I will settle him in my house and in my kingdom for ever; and his throne shall be established for ever. (verses 12-14)

This is toward the latter part of David's reign when he says, "The ark of the covenant of the Lord dwelleth under curtains." That is all the more interesting when you read some of David's Psalms. At least seventy of the Psalms are attributed to David in the book of the Psalms.

Surely goodness and lovingkindness shall follow me all the days of my life; And I shall dwell in the house of the Lord for ever. (Psalm 23:6)

Rabbinic tradition tells us this little Psalm of David's was written when he was a boy. It was one of his earliest Psalms. Where had he gotten such an idea from? There was no real house of the Lord. Again, it is another old Jewish tradition that Jesse was a weaver of the tabernacle veil, and maybe it was in his childhood that David had heard his father saying, "It is about time we had something more permanent for the Lord than this tabernacle which was meant for our wilderness journey." I do not know, but there are other Psalms which show David's clear-sighted understanding of the purpose of God:

Lord, I love the habitation of thy house, And the place where thy glory dwelleth. (Psalm 26:8)

Praise waiteth for thee, O God, in Zion; And unto thee shall the vow be performed. O thou that hearest prayer, Unto thee shall all flesh come. Iniquities prevail against me: As for our transgressions, thou wilt forgive them. Blessed is the man whom thou choosest, and causest to approach unto thee, That he may dwell in thy courts: We shall be satisfied with the goodness of thy house, Thy holy temple. (Psalm 65:1-4)

One thing have I asked of the Lord, that will I seek after: That I may dwell in the house of the Lord all the days of my life, To behold the beauty of the Lord, And to inquire in his temple. For in the day of trouble he will keep me secretly in his pavilion: In the covert of his tabernacle will he hide me; He will lift me up upon a rock. (Psalm 27:4-5)

They shall be abundantly satisfied with the fatness of thy house; And thou wilt make them drink of the river of thy pleasures. For with thee is the fountain of life: in thy light shall we see light. (Psalm 36:8-9)

Thy God hath commanded thy strength: Strengthen, O God, that which thou hast wrought for us. Because of thy temple at Jerusalem, Kings shall bring presents unto thee. (Psalm 68:28-29)

I find that remarkable since there was no temple there. There was something in this man's heart. It is a passion.

Some liberals insist that some Psalms such as these could not have been written by David, that he could not possibly have spoken about the temple. But this thought, that God should have a house, was in the heart of this man from childhood. He had a single eye. It was the passion of his life and he saw in it far more than some house, some place of bricks and mortar of stone and wood and gold and silver and precious stones. He saw in it a pattern of the heavenly. He saw in it something which expressed and illustrated the desire of God to be found amongst His redeemed people.

> *The Lord is in his holy temple; The Lord, his throne is in heaven; His eyes behold, his eyelids try, the children of men. (Psalm 11:4)*

Psalm 18 is a psalm that David wrote when he was delivered from all of his enemies, and in particular, Saul. We know that David wrote this before ever the temple was built and yet he says:

> *In my distress I called upon the Lord, And cried unto my God: He heard my voice out of his temple, And my cry before him came into his ears. (Psalm 18:6)*

> *Lord, remember for David all his affliction; How he sware unto the Lord, And vowed unto the Mighty One of Jacob: Surely I will not come into the tabernacle of my house, Nor go up into my bed; I will not give sleep to mine eyes, or slumber to mine eyelids; Until I find out a place for the Lord, A tabernacle for the Mighty One of Jacob. (Psalm 132:1-5)*

This Psalm 132 was not David's psalm. It was written by others, but it accurately describes the passion of this man's life. I wish to God all of us had such a clear-sighted understanding of the purpose of God. We need it in these days of confusion and perplexity and division and fragmentation. We need clear-sighted understanding of the purpose of God, and what it is He wants to do. David had it. It went right back to his youth and it went right through to the last days of his life.

Perhaps the greatest shock he ever received was when the Lord said to him, "You shall not build Me a house, but your son shall build Me a house."

Trial

The clearer the understanding you have of God's purpose and work, the greater the trial you will have. There were years of trial for David, ending in the throne. At the beginning, it was all so promising. First, David was harp player to Saul and held in great esteem by the king and by the court. Then he defeated Goliath in a most incredible battle, and the whole of Israel said, "Saul has slain thousands, and David his ten thousands" (I Samuel 18:7b). His family was tax-free from then on, and Michal, the king's daughter was given to him as reward for slaying Goliath. He had a close relationship with Jonathan, the king's first-born, heir to the throne. It was all so promising. Then the whole thing plunged into adversity. First came the hatred and malice of Saul, then he had to leave Jonathan, and finally he was being hunted from pillar to post through the wilderness. It was David's trial of faith.

Two times Saul came right into the hand of David. He could have finished him off and taken the throne, and the promise of God through Samuel the prophet, that he should come to the throne, would have been fulfilled. Think of the temptation that must have been! (See I Samuel 24:4-6 and I Samuel 26:7-12) David's men were so excited they said, "Now the time has come for you to take the kingdom," but all David could do was cut off the end of Saul's garment. Then his heart smote him and he said, "I have done evil toward the Lord's anointed. May the Lord forgive me. I will not touch the Lord's anointed." Later on, David could have slain Saul when he was asleep. He could have wakened him and still slain him, so that he would not feel he had killed a sleeping man, but David would not touch him.

If God is ever going to bring you to the throne, He will allow certain things to come your way that will be a great temptation. There will be short cuts to fulfillment, short cuts to rest, short cuts to success, short cuts, in your eyes, to the realization of your ministry. These will not bring you to fulfillment; they will bring you to a tragedy always.

> *That the proof of your faith, being more precious than*
> *gold that perisheth though it is proved by fire, may be*
> *found unto praise and glory and honor at the revela-*
> *tion of Jesus Christ. (I Peter 1:7)*

If we are going to come to the throne, we have to suffer.
If we endure with Him, we shall also reign with Him.

The inner history of these years in David's life is told in a
number of Psalms that you might like to read for yourself
(Psalm 18,34,52,54,56,57,59,63). You will see into the heart of
David, a man that God is disciplining, that God is training,
that God is testing, that God is proving. You will see how
years of trial must end in the throne because there is a character in the man that can do nothing else but reign. There is a
character in that man that must come to the throne. First he
was crowned king of Judah in Hebron, and then later he was
crowned king of all Israel.

Adullam and The Mighty Men

> *David therefore departed thence, and escaped to the*
> *cave of Adullam: and when his brethren and all his*
> *father's house heard it, they went down thither to him.*
> *And every one that was in distress, and every one that*
> *was in debt, and every one that was discontented, gath-*
> *ered themselves unto him; and he became captain over*
> *them: and there were with him about four hundred*
> *men. (I Samuel 22:1-2)*

This cave of Adullam was a formative place in the lives of
all who were with David who finally came to the kingdom. It
is located near the Dead Sea, and they say it is possible to get
four hundred men in it. It is the only large cave in the whole
area which would be safe to take so large a number of men
because it has within it a spring of water. Think of all those
people who were in distress, who were pressurized, who were
discontented. They gathered together to David in the cave of
Adullam, and out of that cave was formed a team that was to
take the kingdom. Those men became the mighty men of
David (see II Samuel 23:8-39). These mighty men were
formed in times of trouble. It could not have been easy for

them. I suppose to us it must have seemed like a sort of pirate's hold-out, but it was not.

Dear friends, may we be preserved from discontented people. Some people join companies of believers such as this through sheer discontent. They have collided with other people and they are fed up to the back teeth with them, so they go somewhere else. But you never get away from anything. If you have collided with someone in a group you have left, you will collide with somebody else wherever you go, only it will be worse. You jump out of the frying pan into the fire. Discontent was never a basis.

But there is a real discontent with things that do not match up to what God really wants. That is a holy discontent. Why should we put up with things that are unscriptural? Why should we put up with things that are erroneous? Why should we put up with things that are compromised and superficial and worldly? To have a holy discontent about that kind of thing is right. God formed those people gathered together at Adullam into a team. It must have been very difficult for them living together, hounded together, pressurized together, like some sort of vast spiritual pressure cooker. They could not get out of it. Something was being done inside of it. So it is when God does anything with us. We have to be beaten into an instrument which God can use to take the throne.

Fighting The Good Fight Of Faith

David was a man of war. I Chronicles 18, 19 and 20 list all the great victories of David over the Edomites, the Ammonites, the Moabites, the Syrians, and the Philistines. All the great traditional enemies of God's people are there and one after another he defeated them. It reminds me so much of those wonderful words of the apostle Paul in one of his last letters, "Fight the good fight of faith, lay hold on life eternal unto which you are called." It does not just come to you willy-nilly. There is a time in this whole matter when you have got to fight the good fight of faith and lay hold on it. There are so many enemies of God, so many enemies of the well-being of God's people, so many of these powers of darkness and the things that are behind flesh and blood.

My heart is fixed, O God; I will sing, Yea, I will sing praises, even with my glory. Awake, psaltery and harp: I myself will awake right early. Be thou exalted, O God, above the heavens, And thy glory above all the earth. Gilead is mine; Manasseh is mine; Ephraim also is the defence of my head; Judah is my sceptre. Moab is my washpot; Upon Edom will I cast my shoe; Over Philistia will I shout. Who will bring me into the fortified city? Who hath led me unto Edom? (Psalm 108:1-2,5,8-10)

For our wrestling is not against flesh and blood, but against the principalities, against the powers, against the world-rulers of this darkness, against the spiritual hosts of wickedness in the heavenly places. Wherefore take up the whole armor of God, that ye may be able to withstand in the evil day, and, having done all, to stand. (Ephesians 6:12-13)

If you and I are going to see the house of God built, we are going to face all the traditional, fierce, violently antagonistic enemies of God's purpose. One after another they will come. They will waylay us one way or the other. Whether from within or without, we shall face enemy after enemy in this whole matter of building. It is not just a matter of the corporate side either. It is personal, because if the enemy can knock you out, he has knocked out one living stone, thereby making the contribution that much less rich. Think of the wait on the whole work when many of us are just knocked out. The enemy comes to us as a company, all the time breathing his lies and insinuations and those phantom things that somehow distance us one from another. How hateful the enemy is! How we need to fight this good fight of faith. We will never see the house of God built or the work of God fulfilled unless we do.

For though we walk in the flesh, we do not war according to the flesh (for the weapons of our warfare are not of the flesh, but mighty before God to the casting down of strongholds), casting down imaginations, and every high thing that is exalted against the knowledge of

God, and bringing every thought into captivity to the
obedience of Christ. (II Corinthians 10:3-5)

When you read that, it is the whole realm that faces us—
satanic strong points, fortresses, strongholds, imaginations. I
find again and again that the thing that lodges in corporate life
is imaginations. People imagine things and you cannot get
those imaginations out. People have speculative reasonings
that need to be cast down! There are high things exalted
against the knowledge of God, not only against the people of
God, but in a town like this, things that hold people in darkness and bondage. Everything begins with thought. Chairman
Mao had a thought. Karl Marx had a thought. It developed
into an ideology which has fettered half the world. All of
these are things that could be brought into captivity to Christ.

Taking Jerusalem

David said, "We *will* take it!" The Jebusites were so
convinced that no one could take Jerusalem that they actually
said, "Except thou take the blind and the lame, thou shall not
come in hither" (see II Samuel 5:6-10) In other words, he will
have to get the lame and the blind out of the way, meaning it
was impossible to take it. Yet the Lord had said to Joshua,
"Every place that the sole of your foot shall tread upon, to you
have I given it." When the men of Joshua's day saw
Jerusalem, they said it was no good. David sent men up
through the old water shaft, they put their feet down on it and
took it. Jerusalem became Zion, *the city of God*. All the way
through David's Psalms you find Zion and Jerusalem. What a
place they hold in his Psalms! He saw that this was the place
where God had caused His name to dwell. This was the place
where the house of the Lord was to be built.

Gathering the Materials

The last thing about this preparation work in David's life
is the gathering of the materials for the house of God. They
were the spoils of war. In I Chronicles 18, we read this very
interesting statement:

And David took the shields of gold that were on the servants of Hadarezer, and brought them to Jerusalem. And from Tibhath and from Cun, cities of Hadarezer, David took very much brass, wherewith Solomon made the brazen sea, and the pillars, and the vessels of brass. And when Tou king of Hamath heard that David had smitten all the host of Hadarezer king of Zobah, he sent Hadoram his son to king David, to salute him, and to bless him, because he had fought against Hadarezer and smitten him (for Hadarezer had wars with Tou); and he had with him all manner of vessels of gold and silver and brass. These also did king David dedicate unto the Lord, with the silver and the gold that he carried away from all the nations; from Edom, and from Moab, and from the children of Ammon, and from the Philistines, and from Amalek. (I Chronicles 18:7-11)

What does this teach us? The house of God is built out of what you and I gain of Christ in the fight of faith. Every time the enemy is beaten, there are spoils of war, and those spoils of war go into the building. How do you grow in grace? You and I grow in the Lord and partake of the divine nature by the exceeding great and precious promises. But how do we often get forced to stand upon those promises? I wish that it was all lovely and easy, but we are all so lazy none of us ever stand on the promises until we have our back up against the wall, until we are at our wit's end, until everything speaks of impossibility. Then we say, "Lord, Lord, I have no one to turn to; what shall I do?" The Spirit breathes a promise into us, we stand on the promise, and God works a victory. We come through that with something of the Lord. We come out with spoils of war, and those spoils of war are gold and silver and precious stones. They are the things that go into the building of the house of God.

Does anything ever come out of defeat? Don't get me wrong, I am not saying that you just go on a crest of victory. Some people have the idea that victory is when the enemy is not there; that you just do not see him; he is gone. Thank God for the times when the Lord removes the enemy so when we go out he is gone. But generally speaking, we know the enemy very near. "We wrestle not against flesh and blood but against principalities." Wrestling is a very indecent, impolite sport. To have a three hundred pound man sitting on top of you is not exactly the most decent thing in the world. Neither is it any sport to have him twisting your arm up your back and nearly tearing it off, or tearing your leg off, or thumping you against some corner. It is not a tennis match. But most people say we are playing a tennis championship match against the powers of darkness, against principalities. We are pitting our skill against them. It is all very decent, very nice, very Wimbledon. No, wrestling is right down to earth, right down on the bottom.

My point is that there are times when the enemy will sit on us. It does not mean that we have lost. It is a wrestling match. There are times when he will pin us down to the ground, when we will have all his weight on top of us, when we will hardly be able to breathe, when we shall feel as if we have some form of spiritual claustrophobia. Nevertheless, by the grace of God and in the name of the Lord our God, we can get up and win, and we can win again and again.

This idea of victory is not something that is all just beautiful. Sometimes we are under, but thank God, we end up on top, and *that is victory*. It is not that you never see the enemy, you never smell the smell of war, but rather that in the midst of it, when you are down, you come out on top. If the enemy pushes you down, the more down you go, the more up you go. Everytime you know the victory of the Lord in such circumstances, you have spoils, and those spoils go into the house of the Lord.

SOLOMON

> *Behold, a son shall be born to thee, who shall be a man of rest; and I will give him rest from all his enemies round about; for his name shall be Solomon, and I will give peace and quietness unto Israel in his days. (I Chronicles 22:9)*

Through Solomon we have the building of the house of God. He is a man of rest, and we know the name, *Solomon,* means "peace." It is the other side of the coin. There can be no building of God's house until all the enemies are defeated. We cannot build the house of the Lord until we have taken ascendency above the enemies of God for they will effectively paralyze the work.

Wisdom

What a need of wisdom there is in building! God appeared to Solomon when he was twenty-one years of age and said, "My son, ask of me and I will give you." Of course, the Lord was testing him again, proving him, and Solomon answered in one of the most beautiful ways in the Word of God:

> *In that night did God appear unto Solomon, and said unto him, Ask what I shall give thee. And Solomon said unto God, Thou hast showed great lovingkindness unto David my father, and hast made me king in his stead. Now, O Lord God, let thy promise unto David my father be established; for thou hast made me king over a people like the dust of the earth in multitude. Give me now wisdom and knowledge, that I may go out and come in before this people; for who can judge this thy people, that is so great? And God said to Solomon, Because this was in thy heart, and thou hast not asked riches, wealth, or honor, nor the life of them that hate thee, neither yet hast asked long life; but hast asked wisdom and knowledge for thyself, that thou mayest judge my people, over whom I have made thee king: wisdom and knowledge is granted unto thee; and I will give thee riches, and wealth, and honor, such as none of the kings have had that have been before thee; neither shall there any after thee have the like. (II Chronicles 1:7-12)*

I do not believe we put enough on wisdom. There is no greater need in the building of God's house than wisdom. You can have the knowledge, but what use? God knows how much knowledge there is; would that there were more. But God knows how much knowledge there is about the doctrine of the church, the technique. People have studied the *Normal Christian Church Life* until they can almost quote it backwards, forwards and upside down. They have the technique, they have the facts. It is true. But wisdom is *how*, and that is the problem. You can know what the church is but *how* to build it, *how* to see it function, *how* to see it produce by the Spirit of God, *how* to see it nurtured, *how* to see it grow up into Christ as Head.

Contributing

We see another thing about the builder himself and it is in this matter of contributing. Solomon had all the wealth that David, his father, had won from battle, and what wealth he had. There were stones of marble, precious stones, stones for inlaid work, iron for the things of iron, brass for the things of brass, silver for the things of silver, gold for the things of gold, and wood in abundance. It was all there.

In the New Testament, Paul wrote of the materials used in building (see I Corinthians 3:10-15). Most of us understand this as our own lives. Is my life wood, hay and stubble or is it gold, silver, or precious stones? But that is not how Paul uses it. He is speaking of himself as a masterbuilder and every man's *work* being tried. That means that everything I have done here or elsewhere will one day be put to the acid test, and it will be clear as to whether my building has been with gold, precious stone and silver or with wood, hay and stubble. The fire will try my ministry.

What are you contributing? What kind of builder are you? The apostle says, "Let everything be done to building up." Perhaps you do not contribute anything. Do not think you will escape, for if you bury your talent it will be taken away from you and given to another. That is what kingship is all about. We are not talking about your salvation, we are talking about reigning. If you have buried what the Lord gave you to contribute and to trade, to exploit in His name, to increase, it will be taken away. You will be saved so as by fire, but what was given to you will be taken away and given to someone else who has known the discipline of God in building. That is why it says again and again, "To him that hath shall be given and to him that hath not shall be taken away even what he hath." He shall be saved so as by fire, but the possibility of reigning, of having dominion being taken away. . .

Eternal Material

Reigning with Christ, overcoming, has very much to do with all this for it has to do with eternal material for an eternal city. It is very easy to have a ministry that is just a matter of words and truths. Anyone with reasonable intelligence can string together some truths, but it is much more when God starts to do a work in you so that there is an anointing, there is a character, there is a capacity, there is a reality. Not one of us who contributes anything can always say that everything we say is true of us. Watchman Nee once said that if we are really being led by God and under the hand of God, then either what we say comes out of what we have learned, or what we say, we shall later learn. God has us under His hand of discipline.

The Building

Then there is the building itself. What a wonderful thing this building is (see II Chronicles 3). First, there was Mount Moriah, the place of the altar, the place of sacrifice, and that is where the house has to be built. It was on the threshing floor of Ornan, the Jebusite. It is there that the house of God has to be built, right on Calvary. You cannot build the house of God anywhere else. It is not a social club; it is not just a question of learning a few doctrines. It has to be built on an experience of Christ crucified, not only as our Savior, but as our representative.

Then notice the massive foundation which they laid, which speaks to us of the one foundation upon which the house of God can be reared and that is Jesus Christ. Staying on the foundation has much to do with overcoming. Sometimes we get pushed off it. We begin to see some ugly things about one another and we say, "I would rather get off this foundation." We do not see the foundation; we see the stones. We have to stay on the foundation. There is only one foundation and we cannot get off of it. We have to go through together.

Living Stones

Then there are living stones. There is no point in living stones unless they are built together. The house is not a heap of stones; it is a number of stones that have found their relationship to one another. Then, over the stones goes silver, over the silver goes wood, and over the wood goes gold. Think of it, all the beauties and glories of Christ! Silver is redemption; wood is the new man; gold is the divine nature. It is wonderful! Finally, into the gold go precious stones, the radiant glories of Christ. It is no wonder to me that in the end the glory of God filled the house, and although Solomon fell away afterwards, with that glory filling the house of God, it is as if the high-water mark in God's program had been reached. Glory.

And the God of all grace, who called you unto his eternal glory in Christ, after that ye have suffered a little while, shall himself perfect, establish, strengthen you. (I Peter 5:10)

"Called to His eternal glory. . ." That is not a personal thing. It is a vessel of glory, it is a house of glory, it is a habitation of glory, it is something to do with union with Christ and union with one another. May God help us in this matter of overcoming. May we go from glory to glory. May we be vessels afore prepared for glory. And if it means that you have to learn how to overcome like David so that you can become a builder, may the Lord do that work in your life and in mine to the fulfillment of His purpose.

OVERCOMING THROUGH HEARING

Elijah

I Kings 19:1-15

I Kings 19:12—And after the fire a still small voice.

Revelation 3:22—He that hath an ear, let him hear what the Spirit saith to the churches.

Elijah was one of the greatest servants of the Lord under the old covenant. He and Moses are taken to represent and symbolize all that the old covenant stood for—Moses, standing for the law and symbolizing the law; Elijah symbolizing and standing for the prophets. In Jewish tradition, both Moses and Elijah have a very, very great place indeed, and it is not some empty tradition. When our Lord was transfigured, it was given to these two servants of the Lord to appear with Him in glory, representing all the saints who overcame in the old covenant.

Although the triumph over the prophets of Baal on Mount Carmel seemed to be the most dramatic and sensational story of his life, Elijah learned the biggest lesson of his life when he fled, in disobedience to the Lord, from Jezebel. The Lord understood Elijah and loved him just as the Lord understands and loves you and me. Elijah flung himself under that juniper and said, "It is enough; now let me die because I really am no better than the rest." The Lord let him fall asleep, and an angel awoke him and fed him without a word of rebuke. He fell asleep again, and we do not know how many hours elapsed. Some have suggested that it was the two meals which we would have called breakfast and an evening meal if he traveled overnight. In the strength of that food, Elijah went forty days and forty nights in the wrong direction. He went farther and farther away from where the Lord wanted him to be, which was in the north in the area of Damascus, to anoint a king.

Finally, when Elijah got to the very end, he came to Horeb. He could not have gone many more miles or he would have gone into the sea because there was no more land. At Horeb he stood before the Lord, and it was then that the Lord spoke to him in reproof, "What are you doing here, Elijah?"

And Elijah began immediately (as all of us do) to rehearse the whole thing in an apologetic way, "Well, Lord, they have cast down Your altars, slain Your prophets, disobeyed You, contravened the covenant, and now I am the only one left, and they are after me."

Then the Lord said to him, "Very well, Elijah, go out and stand on the mount." He went out and stood and he saw three things which summed up his ministry. It must have been the most dramatic exhibition of divine power that anyone could have seen, almost like a divine fireworks display. First, there was a wind that hit the mountainside with such velocity that it split the rocks in two, and there must have been that marvelous sound of falling rocks as well as the hurricane force of the wind. Then there was an earthquake which shook everything but Elijah. Elijah was quite useless. He stood there erect, as far as we can see, and watched the wind and admired the effects of the earthquake as the ground trembled and shook. Finally, there came the fire. And it says the Lord was not in the wind, and the Lord was not in the earthquake, and the Lord was not in the fire.

Those three things summed up Elijah's ministry—wind, earthquake, and fire. There is nothing wrong with wind, earthquake, or fire when it is something spiritual. God has to do some big things in ministry. Without the wind of God there is not much hope. We sing, "Breathe on me, breath of God." Without an earthquake very little ever gets done until many other things that should not be there are shaken down. And without fire there is no power. Nevertheless, there is something far more important than wind, or earthquake, or fire, and it was this that Elijah had to learn that day. After the fire, there was the sound of gentle stillness, or as our older version puts it, "a still small voice." Then the Lord said, "Elijah, what are you doing here?"

The kind of nature we all have is revealed as Elijah trundled out the same apology as before. He was obviously being deeply moved by the still small voice, but he could not help himself. He said exactly the same words again, "Lord, they have done this and this and this, and I only am left; now they are after me."

The Lord did not say another word to him except, "Go. Return."

I think that contains for us one of the greatest lessons that any child of God can learn. The early church had seen the wind of God. It came on Pentecost and it blew like a hurricane force through the Roman Empire. The early church saw the earthquake. It shook the whole traditional institutionalism of Judaism, and finally shook it, in one sense, to pieces. The early church saw the fire. It came on the day of Pentecost and burned everything before it as those great servants of the Lord moved on the roads of the Roman Empire. But when we come to the end of the New Testament we find that the Lord is saying, as it were, to the churches, "Yes, you have had the wind, but I was not in it. It is necessary, but I was not essentially in it. You have had the earthquake, but I was not in it. You have had the fire, but I was not in it. He that hath an ear let him hear what the Spirit says to the churches."

In the end, the most vital lesson that any one of us can learn, the youngest Christian to the oldest and most experienced servant of the Lord, is that to hear the Lord's voice and to obey it is more important than a thousand conferences and a million meetings. What God requires above everything else is a *hearing ear* and an *obedient heart.* We can become so deceived and deluded that we can get entrenched in some excuse and some apology. Then, even when God has really spoken to us and we know He has spoken to us, the old apologetic excuse is still brought out. For this reason, it seems clear to me that the seven churches in Asia, that represented churches all over the world, in time and place, did not hear the Lord when He spoke to them. The result was that by the third century after Christ the whole thing had become formalized, institutionalized and traditionalized with very real errors coming in and taking it all over. The thing had become a vast, universal structure and system. The life had been well nigh killed. It is amazing to me that it is in the Word that the Lord said to every one of those seven churches again and again: *He that hath an ear, let him hear what the Spirit says to the churches.*

He even personalizes it. He does not say, "Let the church hear what the Spirit says to the churches," but He says,

"Let him that hath an ear, hear what the Spirit says to the churches."

There are three things that I want to underline here that have meaning for us at this particular phase in the purpose of God in our day and generation.

THE DIVINE VOCATION FOR MAN

The calling of God for man is that we should have dominion over all things that He has created. That is our divine vocation as man. We are not to be under but to be above, not to be the tail but to be the head, not to be defeated but to overcome, not to be subdued but to subdue. We see it all the way through Scripture.

The Throne of God

First, we see it in *the throne of God,* and what a major part of Scripture is taken up with this whole theme. There are many ways of putting it—the throne of God, the kingdom of God, the ascendancy of God, the rule of God, the administration of God.

We find that the purpose of God is not that you and I should just be servile subjects of His throne; but, that we should be so trained and so conformed to the image of His Son that we should reign from the throne. Furthermore, we should reign from the throne here and now.

> *And raised us up with him, and made us to sit with him in the heavenly places, in Christ Jesus. (Ephesians 2:6)*

That sums up the whole thing. We are not to be the tail; we are to be the head. We are not to be under; we are to be above. It is the very purpose of God that you and I should reach the throne of God, should know what it is to reign with God *now* and be trained in learning how to overcome, how to possess our possessions, how to subdue the enemy, how to nullify his power. In the end we shall be trained for the eternal administration of God. That is really much of what is summed up in the word *kingdom.*

The City of God

Another word we find in Scripture from Revelation 12 to the end of the Bible is the *city of God*, which is described variously. Sometimes it is the city of God, or it is Jerusalem or the new Jerusalem. Sometimes it is the wife of the Lamb, or the bride of Christ. But, however it is viewed it is the same thing. The bride and the wife reveal to us something of the longing of God for an intimacy with us, a love relationship, something that is so sacred, so intimate, so inward. The city of God expresses the desire of God that we should know what it is to reign with Him, to administer His rule, to really know what it is to sit down with the Lord Jesus Christ in His throne. A city is a center of administration. It is the center of government over an area and that is why we find this wonderful theme all the way through the Bible: Jerusalem, the city of God.

The Head and Body

Another way we see it is head and body. The whole point of a body is that it is joined to the head and expresses the mind, the will, and the intelligence of the head. In the New Testament, the most used figure or picture illustrating this relationship of the redeemed and their Lord is that of body to Head. From beginning to end in the Bible we have this thing.

And God said, Let us make man in our Image, after our likeness: and let them have dominion over the fish of the sea, and over the birds of the heavens, and over the cattle, and over all the earth, and over every creeping thing that creepeth upon the earth. (Genesis 1:26)

And God blessed them: and God said unto them, Be fruitful, and multiply, and replenish the earth, and subdue it; and have dominion over the fish of the sea, and over the birds of the heavens, and over every living thing that moveth upon the earth. (verse 28)

The interesting thing here is this word *subdue*. Most people have the idea that when the earth was created there was no need to subdue anything in it. Yet this word *subdue* is the Hebrew word commonly used for subduing enemies, for subduing disorder. You will find it used this way all the way through the Old Testament, and it is interesting that God did not do everything for man. This may be a little clue to what eternity will be like. Some people seem to think it will be boring because there will be nothing to do, there will be nothing to challenge us, nothing to overcome. The fact is that when God created the earth, whilst it was all good, it needed subduing, and there may be very, very much in that word that we as yet do not understand.

> *And the Lord God took the man, and put him into the garden of Eden to dress it and to keep it. (Genesis 2:15)*

That word *keep* is very interesting. We understand *to dress it*, but the Lord put him in the garden *to keep it, to guard it, to watch over it,* and this was before the fall of man.

> *For thou hast made him but little lower than God, And crownest him with glory and honor. Thou makest him to have dominion over the works of thy hands; Thou hast put all things under his feet: (Psalm 8:5-6)*

Some of the modern versions say, "Thou hast given him dominion over all that Thou hast created, and Thou hast put all things under his feet." You have some amazing words here. This word *dominion* is "to cause to rule." *You have caused him to rule over everything you have created and put all things in subjection under his feet.*

This dominion that man was to have was never ever thought of by God as something to be exercised or to be experienced apart from God. In other words, this dominion that man was to have over every single thing He created, to have everything under his feet, was to be in union with God, never apart from Him. It is not self-sufficient dominion.

The interesting thing is that since the fall of man, man has sought to have dominion independently of God, and the whole of human history is this quest for dominion—dominion over natural resources, dominion over things that are wrong, apart from God. Babel is the illustration of this thing in

Genesis 11 when men sought to build a tower that would link heaven and earth. It was the first great attempt to bring heaven to earth and to do it by human endeavor. It was fallen man's genius, this dream that is deep within the human heart to create a Utopia, to create a human paradise, to bring in a golden age, to bring in a kind of millennium, a prosperity and peace, but altogether apart from God. That is Babel.

From then on, throughout the Bible, this word *Babel* represents a whole spiritual idea. It is the word in Hebrew that is always used for the Greek word Babylon. For some reason our translators use the word Babylon, but in the text it is always Babel. It represents human endeavor, human resources, human genius apart from God. It is the attempt of man to have dominion over all things in his own strength and by his own power, with his own wisdom. That is the explanation for human history.

When we come to the time of Daniel, we have the greatest unveiling of the whole of human history from Nebuchadnezzar right down to our own day. We find in Daniel 2 that Nebuchadnezzar had a dream and in that dream he saw a colossus, a vast statue or huge idol. Its head and shoulders were gold, its breast was silver, its thighs were brass, its legs were iron and its toes a mixture of iron and clay. Nebuchadnezzar saw this magnificent statue and saw all the world giving it worship. Then he saw a stone, coming out of the heavens not cut by human hands, hurtling through space toward the statue. It was a small stone which finally hit the statue at its feet, crumbling the whole thing into pieces. Then the stone became bigger and bigger and bigger until it filled the whole world.

No one could understand this extraordinary dream that Nebuchadnezzar had before he was converted. However, Daniel was given understanding of that dream, and you will remember that Daniel told the king that he had seen not only his own empire but the empires that were to follow. In the days of that last great empire, the Roman Empire, there shall come out of heaven this One who is really the Messiah. Through Him, this whole colossus that mankind worships and believes is the epitome of all they could desire, will crumple into ruin and shatter into pieces, and His kingdom shall reign forever and ever. (By the way, this last great empire in

Scripture continues in spirit and in principle right down to western democracy and includes it.)

Later in the book of Daniel (see 7-10), we find that again and again he speaks of certain saints: "And the time shall come for the saints to possess the kingdom." You find this phrase not once but a number of times in those latter visions and dreams that Daniel had. This was God's original design and plan, His vocation for man, that man should have dominion. Man, in union with God, should be the means by which the whole universe was possessed and exploited. The human genius was to be indwelt by the Spirit of God, human creativity indwelt by the Spirit of God. Man was to be empowered by the Spirit of God, ruled by the Spirit of God, broken of any sense of self-importance or ambition, and released to be able to express all the genius God has put within the human being. God, in union with man, would control and govern the whole universe. We do not even know what would have happened if sin had not come in. We just get little glimpses of it where we are told there will come a day when the lion will lie down with the lamb, when the child will play with the poisonous snake, when all the trees and created things will be released from their bondage to corruption into this wonderful, glorious liberty of the sons of God. We do not really know all that God had in mind for this world except that with all its beauty, at present it has been subjected to a cycle of corruption.

God's plan for man never changed when man fell. What happened when man fell? Instead of subduing he became subdued; instead of overcoming he was defeated; instead of being at the head, he went underneath; instead of being over everything, he went under everything. He became a person at the mercy of circumstances, of evil spirits, energized by the spirit of the powers of the air. The father of lies fathered him and something of that poison got into man.

But God has never given up His original plan and design for mankind. Through the redemption which is in Christ, God saves us, He forgives us, He justifies us, He cancels out our sin, He clothes us with the robe of salvation, the garments of righteousness, He makes us a praising people. Tremendous as all this is, it is the smallest part of what God has sought to do through the cross of our Lord Jesus Christ. His aim is to bring us back to the place where we have dominion. That is why God does not come along like some divine nursemaid to continually tide us over every single thing that comes once we begin to grow. He allows problems to come into our lives that would not normally come. All kinds of problems come into the life of a Christian or into a company of real believers with the one express object of teaching them to have dominion. It is because it is far more important to God that you and I should learn how to exercise authority, how to reign with Christ, how to know in experience what it is to sit with Christ in heavenly places, how to know all things in subjection under our feet, how to gain the victory. In other words, God is not going to help us to get victory in a cheap, easy way. He has provided all the grace required for victory in the finished work of Christ, but He is not going to carry us through the battle, as it were. He wants to teach our hands to war; He wants to teach us to have good spiritual muscles because He has eternal vocation in mind.

What would happen if God were to succumb to (if I may so speak of God) becoming sentimental and say, "Poor things, they are crying to Me day and night about this problem they have. I had better remove it." The problem is removed, the issue is removed, the challenge is removed and we get what we want, but we have lost our inheritance. This is what it means in one place in the Scripture where it says:

And He gave them their request, But sent leanness into their soul. (Psalm 106:15)

If you long for idolatry long enough, and God speaks to you once and speaks to you again and speaks to you a third time, He will finally let you go, and you will go into the very center of idolatry. That is what He did with His people. He spoke to them once, twice, three times, and not only did they not listen, they killed His prophets. Finally God said, "Very well, you shall go into the very heart and center of idolatry, into Babylon. Seventy years you shall have of this thing until like some good homeopath you are immunized forever against this idolatry."

The interesting thing is that when it came to going into idolatry the people got so afraid of it. After they had rejected the Lord the third time and He said, "Therefore you shall go in," they began to say, "No, no, no!" They heaped to themselves prophets who would say, "No, of course not. You shall be safe in your own land. God dwells in Jerusalem. This is the house of the Lord. This is where the Lord's name is found." Only Jeremiah stood and said, "You shall go into Babylon because you have not learned your lesson, and you shall stay there seventy years. When you return you will be cured forever of idolatry."

God can give us what we want, but do we want it at that cost? Do you want to have what you want at *that* cost? The children of Israel wanted so much to get out of Egypt, and when they went out, they joyfully despoiled the Egyptians. As the Egyptians handed them their silver trinkets, earrings, rings and necklaces, they just took all they could. It was so exciting getting over the Red Sea and into the land, but within three days in the wilderness, they began to think of Egypt. Before a month, they were longing for the leeks and the garlic and the onions of Egypt. Can you imagine it? They did not think of the promised land and every man sitting under his own vine and under his own olive tree. All they could think of was garlic and leeks and onions.

What a sad thing it is to go back to that, to exchange your promised land, your inheritance forever, for the house of bondage. But do you know there are many of us who are just like that? We would rather be in Egypt in the house of bondage, having a surfeit of onions and garlic and leeks than to be in a promised land.

The strange thing is that in Egypt you have to do everything by hand. Every bit of water has to be pumped up; not a drop comes down. I was in Egypt for two years. The first year, we had ten minutes of rain in the whole year and the second year we had three minutes. Every bit of water had to come by human hand or by some poor donkey. It had to be somehow laborious. But, in the promised land the water came down from heaven. I will never forget Willie Burton's message years ago about onions and leeks and garlic. He said you had to go down to pull up every one of them. Vines and olives come from above; you pick them.

It is a strange thing that some of us would prefer to be in the house of bondage and sweat out all our days bringing up the water. It is human endeavor all the time instead of that which comes down from the heavens. The people of Israel moaned and groaned so much, in spite of the fact that the Lord loved them with all His heart, that He said, "Very well then, if you do not want to go into the promised land, not a single one of you that has murmured against me shall go in. Only Joshua and Caleb shall go over into the promised land."

God sent them into a cycle around the wilderness for forty years until every one of them died because they despised the inheritance of God. Only the two, who would have nothing to do with it but understood that there was an inheritance to obtain through the grace of God, were allowed to go in. They had dominion. They overcame. And you see it in the end epitomized in Caleb when he said, "Give me this mountain." It summed up the whole overcoming spirit of the man. "I do not want the plain; I do not want the desert; I will have that mountain."

Wherever you turn in the Word of God you will find that God wants us to have dominion. He does not just want to redeem us. He does not just want to make us lovely little children, well-dressed and happy. He wants to take us through all those rightful stages to the place where we can exercise dominion. He said to Pharaoh, "Let My son go free that he may serve Me." He spoke of Israel as a son, "My first-born," meaning that there were many other children but Israel was the first-born through which all the blessings should come to the rest of the nations. Remember that. That was God's plan for that people. My point is that the church is to rule and to reign, not in eternity alone, but *now* and we have to learn it *now.*

And he put all things in subjection under his feet, and gave him to be head over all things to the church, which is his body, the fulness of him that filleth all in all. (Ephesians 1:22-23)

There are two wonderful things here. First, Christ is the fulness of all the body. We all recognize that. But the second great truth here is even more remarkable, and not generally understood: the body is His fulness. In other words, Christ wants us together, related together, to be joined to Him in such a way that He can exercise His government and His dominion through us. He wants to express through us, as flesh and blood, the fact that all things are under His feet and that He has been made head over all things to the church. In this sense, His body is His fulness. It is the means by which He expresses the fulness of His government, the fulness of His redemption, the fulness of His power, the fulness of His wisdom, the fulness of His grace. He wants to express it through a vessel, and we are that vessel by grace alone.

> *Now when Jesus came into the parts of Caesarea Philippi, He asked his disciples, saying, Who do men say that the Son of man is? And they said, Some say John the Baptist; some, Elijah; and others, Jeremiah, or one of the prophets. He saith unto them, But who say ye that I am? And Simon Peter answered and said, Thou art the Christ, the Son of the living God. And Jesus answered and said unto him, Blessed art thou, Simon Bar-jonah; for flesh and blood hath not revealed it unto thee, but my Father who is in heaven. And I also say unto thee, that thou art Peter, and upon this rock I will build my church; and the gates of Hades shall not prevail against it. I will give unto thee the keys of the kingdom of heaven: and whatsoever thou shalt bind on earth shall [have been] bound in heaven; and whatsoever thou shalt loose on earth shall [have been] loosed in heaven. (Matthew 16:13-19)*

In other words, "Peter, if you are to know these gates of hell locked up, you have to use the keys of the kingdom of heaven. If there are times when those gates have got to be unlocked so that captives within it can come out into the freedom of the Lord and be saved, you have to use those keys." That is why in chapter 18 we have these words:

> *Again I say unto you, that if two of you shall agree on earth as touching anything that they shall ask, it shall be done for them of my Father who is in heaven. For where two or three are gathered together in my name, there am I in the midst of them. (Matthew 18:19-20)*

We are to have dominion; we are to exercise rule. It sounds all so wonderful until we have to come into the experiences. Whether they are personal, whether they are corporate, whether they are national, God's storms come upon the just and the unjust. In the days of God's judgment, unless He mercifully sends the word for His elect people to be preserved, they suffer along with those who have brought upon them His judgment. In such days, we have to learn how to overcome, how to have the dominion, how to subdue the enemy.

And madest them to be unto our God a kingdom and priests; and they reign upon the earth. (Revelation 5:10)

Now is come the salvation, and the power, and the kingdom of our God, and the authority of his Christ: for the accuser of our brethren is cast down, who accuseth them before our God day and night. And they overcame him because of the blood of the Lamb, and because of 'the word of their testimony; and they loved not their life even unto death. (Revelation 12:10-11)

Do you know what a full salvation is? Why, most of us do not know that a full salvation is salvation and power and the kingdom of our God and the authority of His Christ. I cannot help feeling that if we could learn from the history of the church it would help us greatly. It seems to me that the people of God, at various times, have been at points of great crisis; points when they have not known the full flood of what God has been doing. Then, some point has been reached and almost unknown to them, the departure sets in. If only the people of God had had an ear to hear what the Spirit was saying. In all the preaching and Bible studying and even the prayer meetings, if there had been people who had an ear to hear what the Lord was saying, the whole story of church history could have been different. But the story of church history is that again and again no one has heard. Therefore, in times of crisis, there is no one to stand in the gap, there is no one to build up the wall, there is no one to intercede with God, and His overflowing wrath has come onto the whole.

May I underline this again? The vocation of God is that we should have dominion and He has never ever changed His mind on this thing, nor will. His plan is to bring us to the throne of God and to His city. Dear child of God, such dominion can never come through mere Bible study, or knowledge of doctrine, a Bible college course, a theological degree, or position, or title or even being able to minister the Word of God.

A HEARING EAR

But if the servant shall plainly say, I love my master, my wife, and my children; I will not go out free: then his master shall bring him unto God, and shall bring him to the door, or unto the door-post; and his master shall bore his ear through with an awl; and he shall serve him for ever. (Exodus 21:5-6)

The reason that God bore through the ear was because if you want a servant, you must have his ear. What good is a servant who is the most gifted genius in the whole world if you do not have his ear? The one thing required in a servant is an ear to hear *what* the master says. Sometimes people hear when the Lord shouts loudly enough, but they do not know what He said, only that there was some need. It is amazing to me how God can speak to us and we do not listen to what He says. Sometimes we make our appeal to the Lord both personally and corporately, and we say, "Lord, what shall we do about so and so?" And the Lord will expressly say, "Such and such and such and such," but we do not hear. Sometimes He has to say it again and again, over months; then finally, we wake up and say, "Do you know, I think we are getting what the Lord wants. He said this and this and this." That is why this servant, who was to serve his master forever, had his ear pierced.

Then shalt thou kill the ram, and take of its blood, and put it upon the tip of the right ear of Aaron, and upon the tip of the right ear of his sons, and upon the thumb of their right hand, and upon the great toe of their right foot, and sprinkle the blood upon the altar round about. (Exodus 29:20)

When the high priest and the priest were consecrated, the blood touched the ear first, then the thumb and then the toe. Oh, that God would burn such a lesson into the heart of every one of us! Some of us think it is our toes that need the blood so we can run in the purpose of God. God says, "I do not want your feet, I must get your ears."

Some people say, "Oh Lord, here are my hands. I will work for You." God says that He does not want your hands, it is your ear. *First* your ear, then your hands, then your feet.

And he slew it; and Moses took of the blood thereof, and put it upon the tip of Aaron's right ear, and upon the thumb of his right hand, and upon the great toe of his right foot. (Leviticus 8:23)

And the priest shall take of the blood of the trespass offering, and the priest shall put it upon the tip of the right ear of him that is to be cleansed, and upon the thumb of his right hand, and upon the great toe of his right foot. (Leviticus 14:14)

In this chapter, God tells us of the leper being cleansed by taking the blood of the trespass offering and putting it on his ear. In other words, sin begins with not hearing God. Then it is put on his hand—what he does, what he works, and upon his feet, where he goes. Later, when the leper is cleansed, the blood of the lamb is again put on the ear, upon the thumb and upon the great toe. God is driving home a lesson. Do not put the cart before the horse. It is not the feet or the hands first, but the ear.

Dear Elijah, his feet ran so much, his hands worked so well, and he did hear the Lord. But the greatest lesson of his life was when he found God saying to him, "Elijah, your feet and your hands mean nothing to Me if I do not have your ear."

Sacrifice and offering thou hast no delight in; Mine ears hast thou opened (this literally means, digged; pierced): Burnt-offering and sin-offering hast thou not required. Then said I, Lo, I am come; In the roll of the book it is written of me: I delight to do thy will, O my God; Yea, thy law is within my heart. (Psalm 40:6-8)

God does not require your sacrifice if it is a substitute for your ear. It is your ear that He wants.

My son, If thou wilt receive my words, And lay up my commandments with thee; So as to incline thine ear unto wisdom, And apply thy heart to understanding; Yea, if thou cry after discernment, And lift up thy voice for understanding; If thou seek her as silver, And search for her as for hid treasures: Then shalt thou understand the fear of the Lord, And find the knowledge of God. For the Lord giveth wisdom; Out of his mouth cometh knowledge and understanding. (Proverbs 2:1-6)

Son of man, thou dwellest in the midst of the rebellious house, that have eyes to see, and see not, that have ears to hear, and hear not; for they are a rebellious house. (Ezekiel 12:2)

Hear now this, O foolish people and without understanding; that have eyes, and see not; that have ears, and hear not. (Jeremiah 5:21)

Make the heart of this people fat, and make their ears heavy, and shut their eyes; lest they see with their eyes, and hear with their ears, and understand with their heart, and turn again, and be healed. (Isaiah 6:10)

And thine ears shall hear a word behind thee, saying, This is the way, walk ye in it; when ye turn to the right hand, and when ye turn to the left. (Isaiah 30:21)

Isn't it important to hear that voice? There are times when we can be moving along a course and we fail to hear that voice of the Lord. When we turn, almost unknown to ourselves, we are deviating, either corporately or individually. We fail to hear the voice of the Lord. Our Lord Jesus took this up again and again, *He that hath ears, let him hear. (Matthew 13:9,43)*

You can hear the Lord Jesus saying this again and again. It almost seems to be ridiculous since all those people there had ears. They were hearing His words, they were asking Him questions, but He meant more than physical hearing. Look up the word, particularly in the Old Testament, *Incline thine ear to hear.* You will find it again and again and again. I think there is something in that statement that most of us have not yet understood.

In Revelation 2,3, and 13 you find this word, *He that hath an ear to hear, let him hear what the Spirit says to the churches.* The Laodicean Church had gotten to such a pitch of self-sufficiency, of routine, of good, sound Christian activity, they thought they had everything. They thought they had need of nothing. The Head of the church and the Savior of the body was outside the very door of the church knocking and saying plaintively:

Behold, I stand at the door and knock: if any man hear my voice and open the door, I will come in to him, and will sup with him, and he with me. He that overcometh, I will give to him to sit down with me in my throne, as I also overcame, and sat down with my Father in his throne. He that hath an ear, let him hear what the Spirit saith to the churches. (Revelation 3:20-22)

Do you think it could be possible for a company of believers, Christians, meeting together on good, solid ground, with all their routine and activity to somehow or other, almost unwittingly, push the Lord right outside so that He is outside knocking at the door? It is possible. The lampstand has not yet gone from that church, but the Lord, Who is Head of that church, is outside knocking at the door.

THE OVERCOMER

I will just mention the last thing briefly and trust the Holy Spirit to burn it into your hearts. Wherever you turn in Scripture, you will find this principle. He said that the whole people of God, the whole of Israel should be a kingdom of priests unto Him, but they failed. They set up a golden calf and worshiped it. Then God spoke through Moses and said, "Whoso is on the Lord's side, let him come unto me" (Exodus 32:26). Only the tribe of Levi heard and went to Moses. Then he told them to take their sword and go through the camp, and whether it be relative or friend, to slay them. Right the way through the camp they went, and God said, "I will take Levi for My priest in place of the whole and from this day you shall have no inheritance but Me. I shall be your inheritance, and you shall be the heart of the whole nation, keeping alive My vocation for that nation, keeping alive My purpose for it and keeping alive its true spiritual character. You are the overcomers, not an elite, superior, inner circle. You are those who will lay down your life and have nothing, so that the rest might have everything."

That is an overcomer. People have the idea about overcomer teaching, that it is obnoxious, that it teaches there are first and second-class citizens, that there is a kind of superiority. And there is, in the sense that if you are realizing the purpose of God, *that is superior*. But if we mean by overcoming, some little group of elite people who think they are an establishment that has it and has arrived, and that everyone else has failed and could more or less fail for all we care, that is not overcoming.

The word that saved overcoming for me is this word, "He that overcomes will I grant to sit down in My throne, even as I overcame and sat down with My Father in His throne" (Revelation 3:21). How did our Lord overcome? By laying down His life for the whole. And when He laid down His life for the whole, He laid it down for every single one.

You will find this everywhere in the Word of God. There is Joseph, who was put in a dungeon where the iron might enter into his soul, that he might save the whole of Israel, and finally, all of Egypt as well. There is the remnant that goes back to build the house of God and rebuild Jerusalem in order that the Messiah might come and save the whole world and, in particular, that people. Therefore, the overcomers are not some superior inner circle, but those who like their Lord have let go of their lives in order that He might get the glory and the majority may finally come into the blessing.

There can be no overcoming without hearing the voice of the Spirit of God. Learn then Elijah's great lesson. If you had been to Cherith and to Zarephath and learned the lesson of being cut down, slain and put into the smelting pot, into the crucible of a fiery trial, you might think that you had arrived. If you had been in the contest on Mount Carmel with four hundred false prophets of Baal and only one in the name of the living God, and had seen God come down out of heaven in fire and burn up that offering and four hundred false prophets slain, you might have thought you had arrived. But Elijah learned his biggest lesson after that trial. The voice of one fallen woman put such fear and panic into him that he never heard the voice of God. The panic was so great that God did not even try to speak to him until he was forty days and forty nights into the wilderness. Only then did God speak to him and Elijah learned his greatest lesson. To hear the voice of the Lord is the greatest necessity of all.

This word I have given has personal meaning for us all, and I have no doubt it has local meaning as well as general meaning to the whole church of God. I am sure that there are those of us who have known triumphs of God in our life and in the triumph have lost the voice of God. There are others of us who are perhaps dull of hearing as to what the Lord is trying to say to us. There are things that need to be broken in the name of the Lord, and there are things that we need to understand from God how to deal with in the secret place. So I do trust that we shall not be taken up with the acts of God—wind, earthquake, fire—tremendous as they are, but with the *ways* of the Lord which are essentially a matter of hearing, understanding and obeying the still small voice of God. May the Lord get our ears and help us to hear His voice.

OVERCOMING AND THE RETURNING REMNANT

Zechariah 4:2, 6-9—And he said unto me, What seest thou? And I said, I have seen and, behold, a lampstand all of gold, with its bowl upon the top of it, and its seven lamps thereon; there are seven pipes to each of the lamps, which are upon the top thereof. Then he answered and spake unto me, saying, This is the word of the Lord unto Zerubbabel, saying, Not by might, nor by power, but by my Spirit, saith the Lord of hosts. Who art thou, O great mountain? before Zerubbabel thou shalt become a plain; and he shall bring forth the top stone with shoutings of Grace, grace, unto it. Moreover the word of the Lord came unto me, saying, The hands of Zerubbabel have laid the foundation of this house; his hands shall also finish it; and thou shalt know that the Lord of hosts hath sent me unto you.

Haggai 2:6-9—For thus saith the Lord of hosts: Yet once, it is a little while, and I will shake the heavens, and the earth, and the sea, and the dry land; and I will shake all nations; and the precious things of all nations shall come; and I will fill this house with glory, saith the Lord of hosts. The silver is mine, and the gold is mine, saith the Lord of Hosts. The latter glory of this house shall be greater than the former, saith the Lord of hosts; and in this place will I give peace, saith the Lord of hosts.

Revelation 3:11-13, 21-22—I come quickly: hold fast that which thou hast, that no one take thy crown. He that overcometh, I will make him a pillar in the temple of my God, and he shall go out thence no more: and I will write upon him the name of my God, and the name of the city of my God, the new Jerusalem, which cometh down out of heaven from my God, and mine own new name. He that hath an ear, let him hear what the Spirit saith to the churches. He that overcometh, I will give to him to sit down with me in my throne, as I also overcame, and sat down with my Father in his throne. He that hath an ear, let him hear what the Spirit saith to the churches.

We have been looking at this whole subject of reigning with Christ, or the characteristics of kingship and overcoming. We looked at it first through the whole Bible, a birds-eye view of the whole matter. Then we looked at it as it is illustrated in the lives of different Old Testament saints. Now, we will take a group, and I am going to give them a collective name, underlining one more characteristic of overcoming. Technically, these are the real overcomers because generally speaking, we give the term *overcomer* to those who, when there is general decline and superficiality and things have departed from the mind of the Lord, go right through with God. They give Him the opportunity to do in them what He wanted to do in the whole. In the end, His purpose is realized in and through them and then the rest are brought into it.

So often the idea about the overcomer is that it is some kind of elite inner circle, some kind of little group of in-turned, superior people who look down their noses at all other Christians, but it is not true. The teaching in the Word of God on this matter is that whenever things go wrong, God takes one, or a few, or a number, and through them and the way they have to go, He fulfills His purpose. Then He brings the rest into the blessing. In other words, a person cannot be an overcomer if he thinks he is something elite and superior and better than the others. An overcomer is someone in whom God has done such a work that he is prepared to lay down his life without any thought of reward, without any thought of satisfaction, that the rest may be blessed. God does not want people on the throne who are interested in exhibiting themselves, exhibiting their talents, exhibiting their resources, or even exhibiting what the Lord has done in them and drawing attention to themselves. That is not overcoming. The whole thought of bringing them to the throne is that the universe may be governed for the blessing of all, that others may be blessed, that everything may speak glory, and that the whole universe may be a manifestation of the presence and glory of God.

THE REMNANT

Now we would like to look at this group that we often call *the remnant*. There are many references in the Scriptures to this group, the remnant. If you get a concordance and look up all the references to the word *remnant*, you will be very, very surprised. Isaiah and some of the other prophets spoke again and again about the remnant. In the mind of God, the remnant are those who are going to pay a very full price through their faithfulness and devotion to the Lord. In the end, they will go right through to the throne of God, and because of them then the whole purpose of God can be fulfilled. In one place we are told that the tree will be cut down, but there will be a stump left, and out of the stump there will be a sprout, and from that sprout the whole thing will come to pass. The nation will be cut down, but one will become a thousand and a little one shall become a great nation. It is this whole thought of the Lord reducing right down to a minimum and then fulfilling His purpose through the minimum and bringing the rest into the blessing.

We have it on every side in the Word of God. For instance, we see it in Gideon. He began with thirty-two thousand people, but God said that was far too many. Gideon had to tell everyone who wanted to go home, to go home. (It would be a terrible shock to you if we stood up one day in a meeting and said, "Everyone who is not prepared to be out and out, everyone who is only prepared to come on Sunday for a go-to-meeting type of Christianity, go home; just go home.") Because it is in the Bible we all accept it, but Gideon was told by the Lord to tell everyone who was bothered about home things, domestic things, or anything other than the things of God, to go home. There is no condemnation; you can worship the Lord at home, just go home.

An enormous number went home and ten thousand were left. Then the Lord said to Gideon, "It is still far too many. They will take the glory to themselves. Go down to the brook in Harod and drink. Those who bend down and lap the water up, send them home, but those who cup it up to their mouths, keep."

They were reduced from ten thousand to three hundred. That is the whole point because through the three hundred

God won a tremendous victory over the Midianites and Philistines and brought the whole of Israel into the blessing. All the people that went home came into the blessing of the three hundred, all the ten thousand and all the thirty-two thousand. It was not that there were different levels. God did not say that the twenty-two thousand that went home would get nothing nor the nine thousand and seven hundred that went later.

It is the same principle as when David took his men and some had to stay by the baggage and others went forward. They all came into the reward. That is the principle of the overcomer. Sometimes, some of those who have gone that rather hard way feel a bit bitter and twisted about it. "Why should we have to go this way and then everyone else gets into the blessing? They do not know what it cost us, what it meant to us. They do not know the inner history, the inner battles, the great conflicts, the travail behind the scenes. They do not know anything about that. They have all come into the blessing." But, that is service in the eyes of God.

The remnant that we find spoken of again and again is summed up in people like Zerubbabel, Haggai, Zechariah, Malachi, Ezra, and Nehemiah. They are just a few. If we went back a little earlier we would say, Daniel, Ezekiel, and Jeremiah. These are all part of this same movement of God, what we call recovery.

THE PURPOSE OF GOD

Now there are one or two things here that I want you to understand. First of all, the great majority of the people of God had settled down where they ought *not* to be, and furthermore they were very, very comfortable. They were in Babylon or other places in the whole great complex of Babylonia. The whole nation had been deported by Nebuchadnezzar in three waves of deportations, finally leaving only the poorest of the poor in the land. For seventy years this happened, fifty years of exile. In that fifty years of exile, a remarkable thing happened to the people of God. The problem that had been at the root of their fall had been idolatry, giving worship to things other than God. The prophets had spoken again and again about this matter, warning them that if they had those high places, if they allowed the Baal worship, if they set up those images, if they had the groves through the land, God would judge them. The judgment came and then this remarkable thing happened. The people of God in Babylon were so divorced from their idolatry that from that day to this the Jewish people have never worshiped another idol. It was a homeopathic cure, if you understand homeopathy. Like cures like.

It was as if God said, "I have pleaded with them and pleaded with them; now they will have a dose of it." He sent them to the center of idolatry where they had all the idol worship they could wish all around them. The ministry of Jeremiah began to have its day. Then, even more, the ministry of Ezekiel whose whole great emphasis was on the glory of God departing from the house of God in Jerusalem because of their idolatry, their harlotry, their spiritual adultery, and their compromise over the things of God. God spoke to them through Ezekiel, and they began to understand that they must worship the Lord in purity. They began to study the Word of God for the first time, the law of God came into its place, they began to make the distinction between unclean and clean foods, they began to watch very carefully on the Sabbath, and they began to have meeting places, which we now call synagogues. This all began at that time. They began to build these simple little places where the Word of God could be read, studied, interpreted and expounded, where matters of behavior and conduct and routine life, as well as the things of the kingdom could be settled.

As always, the people of God, through much affliction, began to prosper, and before very long (if we believe archeology), the banking houses were in their hands, as well as a number of other things in Babylon. They began to prosper and prosper. They had schools. They had their own freedom of worship. Everything seemed so right; but you see, the purpose of God could never be fulfilled in Babylon. How could the word of the prophet Isaiah be fulfilled that Galilee of the nations would see a great light?

For unto us a child is born, unto us a son is given; and
the government shall be upon his shoulder: and his

*name shall be called Wonderful, Counselor, Mighty
God, Everlasting Father, Prince of Peace. (Isaiah 9:6)*

How could it be fulfilled if there was no Galilee? How
could a virgin conceive and bear a son and call His name
Immanuel if there was no Galilee?

Listen to the prophet Micah also prophesying before the
captivity when he said:

*But thou, Bethlehem Ephrathah, which art little to be
among the thousands of Judah, out of thee shall one
come forth unto me that is to be ruler in Israel; whose
goings forth are from of old, from everlasting. (Micah
5:2)*

How could it be fulfilled? Bethlehem had been razed to
the ground; its population had been deported. There was no
Bethlehem. How could the words of Isaiah about Jerusalem
being built up and Jeremiah's word about them returning
again be fulfilled? How could it be fulfilled in Babylon? It
could not be fulfilled in Babylon! You could know the Lord in
Babylon; you could be saved by the grace of God in Babylon;
you could study the Word of God in Babylon; you could grow
in the knowledge of the Word of God in Babylon; you could
be devoted to the Lord in Babylon; you could be separated
from the world in Babylon; you could have a real relationship
with the Lord and with your brothers and sisters in Babylon;
but, the purpose of God could never ever be fulfilled in
Babylon. That is the crux of the whole matter. One of the
most beautiful little Psalms was written coming out of that experience:

*By the rivers of Babylon, There we sat down, yea, we
wept, When we remembered Zion. Upon the willows
in the midst thereof We hanged up our harps. For
there they that led us captive required of us songs, And
they that wasted us required of us mirth, saying, Sing us
one of the songs of Zion. How shall we sing the Lord's
song in a foreign land? If I forget thee, O Jerusalem,
Let my right hand forget her skill. Let my tongue
cleave to the roof of my mouth, If I remember thee not;*

If I prefer not Jerusalem above my chief joy. (Psalm 137:1-6)

You see, there was a small remnant in Babylon who had seen something of the purpose of God. As they studied the Word of God and as the Spirit of God threw light upon it, they came to see, that in some way everything was related to Jerusalem. It was related to the rebuilding of the house of God, to the rebuilding of Jerusalem, to the rebuilding of Bethlehem, to the rebuilding of Galilee, and someone had to pay the price and go back.

THE RETURN

There were three returns. The first return was under the decree of Cyrus, under the leadership of Zerubbabel in 537 B.C., the second return was under the leadership of Ezra in 458 B.C., and the third return was under the leadership of Nehemiah in 445 B.C. The dates of these returns are very important to my point. Here is the reason why. Everyone loves the book of Esther; but, the rabbis had tremendous discussions about whether the book of Esther should even be in the Bible. That discussion continued right up to the second century after Christ because the book of Esther not once mentions the things of God, not once mentions the Word of God, not once mentions anything about the purpose of God. It seems to be a heathen book. Actually, in Hebrew, there are four turning points in the history of Esther; four turning points with acrostics in Hebrew which spell the name of the Lord. Isn't that wonderful? There are four turning points where, hidden in the record, is the name of the Lord.

We love the story of Esther, how the Lord brought her to the throne and saved all those people in the dispersion by her. Esther comes in between the first and the second return, between 486 B.C. and 465 B.C. Now my whole point is that God was prepared to deliver all the Jews who did not return. He was prepared to save them; He was prepared to exhibit and express His mighty arm in their deliverance; but, their deliverance had absolutely no effect whatsoever on the purpose of God. If every Jew in Babylon had died, it would not have meant one single digit of difference to the purpose of God being fulfilled because God had got the remnant back! One of the edicts passed was that if there were Jews in sufficient number, they could arm themselves and withstand attack; otherwise they could be massacred. The only place where there were Jews in sufficient numbers, trained and hardy enough, was Jerusalem. They were the ones who had gone back; they were pioneers.

THE COST

There are three kinds of Christians in Christian circles. There are those who have absolutely no idea whatsoever of the purpose of God. They are the kind of people that would come to a place like this or any other company of people (there are a number of them all over the world) and would just look upon it as a church or a chapel, nothing more, nothing less. They do not understand anything of the history. There are people who may even come regularly who have absolutely no idea. Their vision goes up to a certain point, getting people saved, or perhaps even to holiness or to the charismatic, or maybe even beyond gifts to something else in service, but they do not really see the purpose of God. For them it is just the point of going where you get a bit more life, a bit more teaching and a little bit more informality and warmth. That is all that really matters. There are a large number of people who are saved, thank God, who know the Lord, thank God, but who have no idea as to the purpose of God; why God has saved us, what He is driving at, or what is the object of His purpose.

The second group of people are those who do know what the Lord's purpose is. They could even give you so many points on it. They are the people who can sort of spout the Scriptures; they can define the purpose. "The purpose of God is to present the bride to His Son. The purpose of God is to build the house of God so that the topstone can come upon it. The purpose of God is to build living stones together." They know it in the head, but they will not yield themselves to the Lord. They are not prepared to pay the price. There are many, many people like this, who are prepared to go right along with it. They have seen something, but they have issues in their lives that they will not allow God to deal with.

The third group are the people who, having seen the purpose of God, commit themselves lock, stock, and barrel to that purpose, and it means a tremendous amount the way they have to go. Those who come to the throne of God have been made, by the grace of God, an integral part of His purpose. They have paid the price. They have been prepared to go back, they have been prepared to go the whole way with the Lord whatever the cost, they have been prepared for the discipline of being built together, the discipline of being related, the discipline of being under authority and all these other things. Because they are prepared to pay that kind of price, they have become an integral part of the fulfillment of God's purpose. That is why they are overcomers. Through them the Lord fulfills His purpose.

Many of us are quite happy to live in a state of things, Christian-wise, which is anything but what God wants. We know it. We see all of our top-heavy organizations, all our dead formality, all our systems that we have inherited. We know very well that if God is really going to get His way, it is going to mean the turning over of the whole thing.

Those folks who went back had no synagogues. They had no comfortable places where they could just sit and study the Word of God. If you read the story of Ezra and Nehemiah, if you read the prophecies of Haggai, Zechariah and Malachi, you find that they had to stand with sword in one hand and trowel in the other. There were men like Sanballat and Tobiah and Geshem, the Arabian. Some of them had a bit of Jewish blood in them. They wanted to come right in on the work and bring into it all the compromise of the Samaritans: "Why do you have to be so legalistic? Why do you have to be so one hundred percent? Why do you have to be so absolute? Let us join in."

But Nehemiah said, "Never!" and then began all the problems.

I must tell you that to follow the Lord in this way costs you infinitely more than just settling down into something which is other than the Lord's mind, but which the Lord will bless. Some people have got the strangest ideas about this. They say, "But the Lord should not bless it," and "It must be the devil."

My dear friends, God blesses His children wherever He finds them. When He finds born again believers, He will bless them anywhere. Some people feel that the Lord could not possibly save a Catholic, especially if that Catholic went on being a Catholic; he should become an Anglican. The Baptists feel that the Lord could not bless Anglicans with all that business about infant baptism. Impossible! If anyone is going to go on with the Lord they will be out of Anglicanism in a moment. Then you have the Brethren and they feel if you are going to go on with the Lord, you will be out of the Baptists in no time. You can't have any freedom around the Lord's Table. Then you have the Charismatics. (Thank God for the Charismatics.) They say you ought to be out of all that lot or the Lord will turn it upside down if He gets inside. One of the most wonderful things is that God *has* turned things upside down. Fifteen or twenty years ago things that we would have said were impossible, God has done them. It is not now a question of our geographical location as such. It is a question of the dimension we are in spiritually, whether we are committed to the fulfillment of God's purpose or not, whether we are prepared for whatever the cost will be in order that God should have His way.

The Lord has said, "Not by might, nor by power but by my Spirit says the Lord of hosts." There were two olive trees, one on either side of the lampstand. One spoke of kingship, the other spoke of priesthood, two great ministries. If we are going to see this job done, we have got to reign with Christ *now*.

You know, Zerubbabel was a king in spirit. It would have been much easier for him, with his leadership qualities, to stay in the comfortable atmosphere of Babylon, going around speaking at all of the synagogues, expounding the Word of God. But how do you expound Micah 5, when there is no Bethlehem?

This is the funny thing in Christian circles, we can expound things. I remember some years ago listening to a brother who gave us the most amazing address on the nature of the church. The thing that so amazed me was that in the denomination he came from hardly a single thing of it was true. I was very interested. I had no idea that he believed this. When I asked him about how he reconciled it with the practice of the particular group he was in, he said, "You see, brother, the doors would have closed against my ministry if I had preached *this* there." That is *not* overcoming. If I think my ministry is more important than the house of God, where am I?

It is an incredible thing to me, when I go to some theological seminaries, to hear that the students are being taught how to keep their congregation and how to get their support. In the end, one feels that the congregation is the backdrop for the minister. It is the stage upon which he preaches. They are there for him, and therefore the ministry is more important than the end. But the ministry has an end, and that end is the house of God. The house of God should be so built that it can build up itself in love and increase with the increase of God and not be dependent on big ministries.

I want to ask you a question. Is your spiritual experience in the book of Esther or is it in the book of Nehemiah? Where are you? Now do not get me wrong on this matter. God does not hold it against those who do not go back. He does not withdraw their salvation. He does not curse them. He works wonderful deliverances on their behalf. Sometimes, some of the things the Lord does in the Babylonian state of affairs are more wonderful than some of the things He seems to do in the land; but, those folks will never become part of the fulfillment of God's purpose. Saved? Yes, but not brought to the throne. That is what I want to put my finger on here.

Overcoming is not just a matter of our relationship one to another. It is a matter of faith, overcoming faith. It is a matter of life, overcoming life. It is a matter of the transformation of our character, of our beings, by the renewing of our mind. It is the tasting of the fellowship of Christ's sufferings. It is a matter of inheriting. All these things are personal things; but then, it becomes a matter of the house of God. We saw that in David and Solomon and we see it even more here. We have those wonderful words from Isaiah that the Lord would say to Cyrus, "Jerusalem shall be built and the foundation shall be laid." Those words were uttered before they ever went into captivity, before the exile even took place. It was a remnant that was going to be used by God to do that.

Dear child of God, I am not asking for any elite, superior circle. It is a matter of whether you are prepared to lay down your life for Him and commit yourself to His way, whatever the cost. May we be like those in Psalm 126:1-6:

> *When the Lord brought back those that returned to*
> *   Zion,*
> *We were like unto them that dream.*
> *Then was our mouth filled with laughter,*
> *And our tongue with singing:*
> *Then said they among the nations,*
> *The Lord hath done great things for them.*
> *The Lord hath done great things for us,*
> *Whereof we are glad.*
> *Turn again our captivity, O Lord,*
> *As the streams in the South.*
> *They that sow in tears shall reap in joy.*
> *He that goeth forth and weepeth, bearing seed for*
> *   sowing,*
> *Shall doubtless come again with joy, bringing his*
> *   sheaves with him.*

Oh, how wonderful it will be when God has worked such a character in us by His Spirit in this whole matter of reigning with Christ, of overcoming, of the recovery of the house of God and its being built to receive the topstone! We shall not think of ourselves, of our own satisfaction, of our own glory or our own reward, or our own position. But our only interest will be in the Lord Himself, and in the people of God, their blessing, their glory, their building up, and the world that it might be saved. If God could get such a character as that, the eternal government of the universe in the ages to come is absolutely safe. May the Lord help us that we may overcome as our Lord Jesus has overcome.

JESUS THE OVERCOMER
KING OF KINGS

Deuteronomy 28:1-14

Verses 13-14—And the Lord will make thee the head, and not the tail; and thou shalt be above only, and thou shalt not be beneath; if thou shalt hearken unto the commandments of the Lord thy God, which I command thee this day, to observe and to do them, and shalt not turn aside from any of the words which I command you this day, to the right hand or to the left, to go after other gods to serve them.

Luke 22:29-30—And I appoint unto you a kingdom, even as my Father appointed unto me, that ye may eat and drink at my table in my kingdom; and ye shall sit on thrones judging the twelve tribes of Israel. (I now vest in you the kingship which my Father vested in me. NEB)

Luke 12:32—Fear not, little flock; for it is your Father's good pleasure to give you the kingdom.

I want us to consider here the Lord Jesus as **THE** overcomer. We are to overcome as He has overcome. In fact, the key to all overcoming, both its nature and its power, is in that one fact that Jesus is **THE** overcomer. It is in our relationship to Him and our experience of Him, being conformed to His image and really walking in the way that He walked, that we shall know Him overcoming in us again.

He that overcometh, I will give to him to sit down with me in my throne, as I also overcame, and sat down with my Father in his throne. He that hath an ear, let him hear what the Spirit saith to the churches. (Revelation 3:21-22)

These things have I spoken unto you, that in me ye
may have peace. In the world ye have tribulation: but
be of good cheer; I have overcome the world. (John
16:33)

Do you see the connection there of being in good cheer
and His overcoming the world? Why should that cheer us up?
In one way it might even depress us. He has overcome, we
have not. He is at the right hand of God, the Father; we are
down here on earth at the mercy of the enemy, seemingly.
Why did the Lord say, "In the world you shall have tribulation"? In other words, He is not giving us a rosy picture. "In
Me you shall have peace, in the world you have tribulation:
but be of good cheer; I have overcome the world." There is a
connection between His overcoming the world and our overcoming.

In Acts 14:22 it says that through much tribulation we
enter into the kingdom of God, or to put it another way,
through much tribulation we are prepared for kingship. We
enter into our place as those who can reign with Christ. So we
have tribulation in the world and peace in the Lord Jesus
Christ, but we are to be of good cheer because He has overcome the world.

For whatsoever is begotten of God overcometh the
world: and this is the victory that hath overcome the
world, even our faith. And who is he that overcometh
the world, but he that believeth that Jesus is the Son of
God? (I John 5:4-5)

Our overcoming is connected with a living relationship to
the Lord Jesus, a living appreciation of the Lord Jesus, a living
recognition of the Lord Jesus.

Nay, in all these things we are more than conquerors
through him that loved us. (Romans 8:37)

It is not just that in all these things we are conquerors, or
in all these things we get through, but in all these things we are
more than conquerors. The New American Standard Bible

puts it like this: "In all these things we overwhelmingly conquer." How do we overwhelmingly conquer? It is through Him that loved us. All overcoming is through Jesus, the overcomer. It is connected with His Person and with His overcoming.

> *But thanks be unto God, who always leadeth us in triumph in Christ, and maketh manifest through us the savor of his knowledge in every place. For we are a sweet savor of Christ unto God, in them that are saved, and in them that perish. (II Corinthians 2:14-15)*

> *But thanks be to God, who leads me on from place to place in the train of His triumph, to celebrate His victory over the enemies of Christ, and by me, sends forth the knowledge of Him, a stream of fragrant incense throughout the world, for Christ is the fragrance. (Conybeare's translation)*

Paul is borrowing a picture from those great triumphant Roman generals who went back to Rome and in their train, they took all their captives, all the kings, all the nobles, all the big people. They had to trail behind those Roman generals in their great procession of victory; and he says that is what happened to us. We are in the train of Christ's triumph. We are in His triumphal procession. He is the overcomer, and we overcome because of His overcoming.

> *But thanks be to God, who giveth us the victory through our Lord Jesus Christ. (I Corinthians 15:57)*

If we are to come to the throne, if we are to reign with Christ in eternity, we must follow Him in the path that He trod to the throne. There is no other way to the throne of God and there are no short cuts. If we would sit down with the Lord Jesus in His throne, we must understand how He came to the Father's throne.

> *Verily, verily, I say unto you, Except a grain of wheat fall into the earth and die, it abideth by itself alone; but if it die, it beareth much fruit. He that loveth his life*

*loseth it; and he that hateth his life in this world shall
keep it unto life eternal. If any man serve me, let him
follow me; and where I am, there shall also my servant
be; if any man serve me, him will the Father honor.
(John 12:24-26)*

If you want to go to the place where the Lord Jesus is in
the Father's throne, you have to follow the path He trod to
that throne. There is no escaping; there is no by-passing. We
have to go the same way. Jesus lost His life; He hated His life
and kept it unto life eternal. He was prepared to lay down His
life for the Father and for our salvation, our redemption. We
must follow the same way because there is no possibility of
fruit and no possibility of a harvest unless we can fall into the
ground and die. That is our problem.

*He that saith he abideth in him ought himself also to
walk even as he walked. (I John 2:6)*

What does it mean to abide in Christ? The Lord Jesus
was at great pains to speak to us again and again in the last
moments of His earthly life about abiding in Him. It means
that if we abide in Him we are to walk as He walked, follow in
the path that He trod.

*For hereunto were ye called: because Christ also suf-
fered for you, leaving you an example, that ye should
follow his steps. (I Peter 2:21)*

Christ had to overcome what we have to overcome. We
sometimes forget that. What do you and I have to overcome?
We have to overcome the world, the devil and the flesh. That
is exactly what the Lord Jesus had to overcome, nothing less
and nothing more.

Jesus Overcame the World

Jesus said, "Be of good cheer, I have overcome the
world." What did the Lord Jesus mean by the world? Did He
just mean the natural creation? Of course not! We were
meant to have dominion over the natural creation and we

have lost it very largely. Now, by the sweat of our brow, we just keep our heads above water. It was far more that the Lord meant when He said, "I have overcome the world." He meant that whole world order of inverted values, that puts all the emphasis on the transient and no emphasis upon the eternal. That world order believes that the way to the throne is always to push others down, to be forceful, to grab things, grasp things, fight for things. It is jealously, rivalry, hatred, malice. But not only that, there are many good things about this world order, too. There are things that can just as easily unseat us because they are beautiful and seemingly noble and have great ideals. We do not look to whether they have foundations.

Jesus Overcame the Devil

Now is the judgment of this world: now shall the prince of this world be cast out. (John 12:31)

How is the devil cast out? He was cast out when Jesus was crucified on the tree. By dying, He brought to nought him that had the power of death and delivered them who all through life were subject to bondage through fear of death (see Hebrews 2:14-15).

Jesus Overcame the Flesh

Perhaps you wonder how Jesus overcame the flesh because there was no sin in His flesh. He did not have the kind of flesh that we have, but the Lord Jesus also overcame the flesh. We make a great mistake if we only think of sin in our flesh. There is a self-life which has to be overcome. Let us look at just two scriptures that may put this in perspective.

For we have not a high priest that cannot be touched with the feeling of our infirmities; but one that hath been in all points tempted like as we are, yet without sin. (Hebrews 4:15)

*For in that he himself hath suffered being tempted, he
is able to succor them that are tempted. (Hebrews
2:18)*

Evidently, the Lord Jesus knew something about the
temptations that came along the line of His self-life. Although
He was without sin, He faced a testing such as none of us will
ever face and He overcame it all. Now, in us, He will overcome again. He will overcome the world in me, in you; He
will overcome the devil in me, in you; He will overcome the
flesh in me, in you.

KEYS TO CHRIST'S OVERCOMING

There are a number of keys to Christ's overcoming that
are a tremendous help to us. I am going to give you four keys
to the overcoming of Christ that are of tremendous help and
value to us. They are essential if we are going to know what it
is to be overcomers.

UNION WITH THE FATHER

Christ would do nothing from Himself. I wonder if you
have ever noticed this matter recorded and emphasized in
John's gospel. The Lord Jesus *spoke* everything out of union
with His Father, *worked* everything out of union with His
Father, *willed* everything out of union with His Father.
Always! The perfect Son of God, the Son of Man who was
holy, blameless, separate from sinners, without sin and yet He
said again and again, "I do nothing from Myself." Why can
He do nothing from Himself? There is no sin to mar, there is
nothing to spoil, there is no iniquity, no transgression in Him.
Why does He not just spontaneously do everything out from
Himself? No, Jesus would do nothing from Himself.
Do not always hide behind sin. Even if you and I had
never sinned (and there is not one of us in that category), we
could still spoil everything by simply doing things out from
ourselves. The key to Jesus' overcoming was union with His
Father. Even as a sinless Man, even as the One who was
absolutely holy, everything had to be out from the Father.

Jesus therefore answered and said unto them, Verily, verily, I say unto you, The Son can do nothing of himself, but what he seeth the Father doing: for what things soever he doeth, these the Son also doeth in like manner. (John 5:19)

Isn't that an incredible statement? One of our first great lessons in kingship from the life of Abraham was, "Whatsoever is begotten of God overcometh the world." Everything must originate in God if it is to go through to the kingdom. If it is to inherit the promises, it has to begin with God.

I can of myself do nothing: as I hear, I judge: and my judgment is righteous; because I seek not mine own will, but the will of him that sent me. (John 5:30)

Why does the Lord Jesus say this? It is because He only seeks the will of Him that sent Him. Therefore, because He wants to do the will of the Father, He will do nothing out from Himself. Now do not get the idea that Jesus was a passive doer of nothing. The Lord Jesus spent His whole time doing good—healing the sick, casting out the demons, cleansing the lepers, raising the dead on a number of occasions. He was constant movement, all the time everywhere. But He describes the whole thing by saying, "I can of Myself do nothing. I seek only the will of Him that sent me."

Jesus therefore said, When ye have lifted up the Son of man, then shall ye know that I am he, and that I do nothing of myself, but as the Father taught me, I speak these things. And he that sent me is with me; he hath not left me alone; for I do always the things that are pleasing to him. (John 8:28-29)

For I spake not from myself; but the Father that sent me, he hath given me a commandment, what I should say, and what I should speak. (John 12:49)

In other words, when the Lord Jesus spoke, it was out from union with His Father. Do not think for a moment that it was some kind of legal bondage the Lord Jesus was in, some kind of inhibition, always nervous as to whether He could speak or could not speak. It was spontaneous, but it was from union with the Father so that He spoke the words of His Father, He did the will of His Father.

> *Believest thou not that I am in the Father, and the Father in me? the words that I say unto you I speak not from myself: but the Father abiding in me doeth his works. (John 14:10)*

What an unfolding revelation of union with God! "I can do nothing of myself," ends with, "the Father abiding in me doeth his works." If only we knew something like this, not being able to do anything from ourselves. If we only knew positively, Christ in us doing His works. That is overcoming. Now you begin to realize that to overcome is really a matter of union with the Father. That is why the Lord Jesus said, "Abide in me and I in you."

Have you ever really looked at the temptations of Jesus in Matthew, chapter 4? Some of those things the devil tempted the Lord Jesus to do did not seem to be so terrible. What is so bad about turning a stone into a bit of bread, especially if it could be given to somebody? The devil came to the Lord Jesus and said, "Turn this stone into bread." Would the whole of heaven have collapsed if Jesus had said, "Stone, be bread"? Then, when it was bread, He could have said to someone, "Take that to so-and-so, they are hungry."

Would it have really been so terrible if Jesus had thrown Himself off the pinnacle of the temple? He did enough other things that were exciting. Raising up Lazarus from the dead must have been a tremendous excitement, especially when he was four days dead. It caused such a fuss in the Sanhedrin that they actually met together to see what they could do to Lazarus to put him back into that tomb. They never questioned the miracle; it was the evidence they were worried about. The Lord Jesus did some amazing things. What then would be so terrible about throwing Himself off the pinnacle of the temple?

The last temptation was when the devil said, "Bow down to me; I will give you all this." That is where the colors of the enemy came out into the open. What was the enemy trying to do? He was trying to get Jesus to do things out from Himself. Satan knew very well that the only way Jesus, as the Son of Man, could overcome was to keep in union with His Father. If once he could get Him to turn stone into bread for good purposes, but from Himself, he had Him. Satan tried to give Jesus a short cut to recognition by throwing Himself off the pinnacle of the temple. By the way, the pinnacle of the temple was in the most crowded part of the city. It is not so today. When you look over the pinnacle of the temple there does not seem to be anything there. So people tend to think that there was not anything so marvelous about this because only a few people going by on donkeys would have seen Him. But in those days, the really crowded, poorer part of the city was all under those walls. If He had cast Himself off the pinnacle, it would have been a tremendous sight as angels carried Him down.

Many of us get caught on this thing. In the service of God we get caught on doing things that are good. We get into a tremendous routine of activity and doing things which are good, turning stones into bread, and it is not out from union with the Father. Therefore, we do not overcome. I know people who will do all kinds of things to try and help things along, to get them off the ground a bit, sort of get things going. It is like jumping off the pinnacle; it is trying to get that short cut to popular recognition.

Then the enemy said to Him on the third try, "Look here, bow down just once. I do not want You to do it forever, just once. If you bow down once and worship me, I will give You all the kingdoms of the world."

Jesus never questioned the fact that the kingdoms of the world were under the authority of Satan. It could have been another short cut. That is what the enemy is doing to you and me all the time. Jesus said, "Abide in Me." That is all. There is no way to overcoming except through dependence upon Christ, union with Christ. As the Lord Jesus acted out from union with the Father, so we act out from union with Him. Everything must be of Christ.

Wherefore if any man is in Christ, he is a new creature: the old things are passed away; behold, they are become new. (II Corinthians 5:17)

For to me to live is Christ, and to die is gain. (Philippians 1:21)

For ye died, and your life is hid with Christ in God. When Christ, who is our life, shall be manifested, then shall ye also with him be manifested in glory. (Colossians 3:3-4)

I have been crucified with Christ; and it is no longer I that live, but Christ liveth in me: and that life which I now live in the flesh I live in faith, the faith which is in the Son of God, who loved me, and gave himself up for me. (Galatians 2:20)

Now on the last day, the great day of the feast, Jesus stood and cried, saying, If any man thirst, let him come unto me and drink. He that believeth on me, as the scripture hath said, from within him shall flow rivers of living water. (John 7:37-38)

Abiding in Christ

Where do rivers of living water come from? They come from Christ within. They are not something in yourself; they are something in Christ. He is the well, springing up unto life eternal that comes into us by the Spirit of God. This whole matter is really tremendous when we begin to see it in terms of abiding.

Abide in me, and I in you. As the branch cannot bear fruit of itself, except it abide in the vine; so neither can ye, except ye abide in me. I am the vine, ye are the branches: He that abideth in me, and I in him, the same beareth much fruit: for apart from me ye can do nothing. (John 15:4-5)

We can do an awful lot without Christ. Many of us have learned it through bitter experience. We can preach without Him; we can pray without Him; we can work without Him; we can witness without Him; we can have meetings without Him; we can go through all kinds of activity without Him; we can do a tremendous amount without Him. What did He mean? Apart from Christ there is nothing that goes through to the kingdom. You can spend your whole time in a round of activity, but unless it is out of union with Him, it does not reach the throne. It does not come into the kingdom.

> *If ye abide in me, and my words abide in you, ask whatsoever ye will, and it shall be done unto you. Herein is my Father glorified, that ye bear much fruit; and so shall ye be my disciples. Even as the Father hath loved me, I also have loved you: abide ye in my love. If ye keep my commandments, ye shall abide in my love; even as I have kept my Father's commandments, and abide in his love. These things have I spoken unto you, that my joy may be in you, and that your joy may be made full. This is my commandment, that ye love one another, even as I have loved you. (John 15:7-12)*

When our Lord Jesus came to the last moments of His earthly life, He put all the emphasis on this little sentence, "Abide in me and I in you." He said it again and again and again. That is the secret. It is the secret to victory; it is the secret to reigning with Christ here, now, and it is the secret to reigning with Christ in eternity to come. It is the secret to overcoming. We must learn therefore to abide in Him .

Doing God's Will

> *And the world passeth away, and the lust thereof: but he that doeth the will of God abideth for ever. (I John 2:17)*

What is the will of God for your life? Maybe you have some issue. He is saying something to you and there is battle over it. Perhaps you have had years of battle over it. It is simple just to do it and you will abide forever. Overcoming is just doing the will of God in the simplest matters. It will lead you to the greatest consequences. People get all tied up on huge matters, and all God is saying to them is, "Do this; you do it, you abide forever." Something goes into the kingdom. It is the way.

When C.T. Studd lay dying (and in the end he could only gasp a little), they asked him if he had anything to say. He said, "I can only say that of all the Lord has ever asked me to do, I have done every single thing."

I think that is the most wonderful way to end one's life. God does not bother you about the things He did not ask you to do. Do not think God is going to hold you responsible for the millions in China if He did not call you to China. But if He spoke to you about speaking to your neighbor across the road and you did not, He does hold you responsible. We get all heated up about something on the other side of the globe or some great tragedy that is taking place in some company of believers. It is not wrong to get burdened, but really what God is simply saying is: "You are not to bother about that. It is My business. I have not called you to that. I have told you to do this and this and this. You do it and if you do it, you will come into great blessing."

Walking in Afore Prepared Works

Another matter that we need to touch on here is not only that we abide in Him and do His will, but also that we walk in "afore prepared works."

For we are his workmanship, created in Christ Jesus for good works, which God afore prepared that we should walk in them. (Ephesians 2:10)

God has works He has afore prepared. The trouble with many of us, if not all of us, is that we are doing works of our own making. They are not His works; they are our works. They may be good Christian works. They are sometimes needful works, but they are not works afore prepared that we should walk in them. If you want to overcome, you must stay in the works afore prepared. Oh, what a discipline it is for us who are in the service of God in any measure to know this. When we are called to this side, that side, the other side, what should we do? We can get into a spiral of activity. We get called here and there; here is a need, there is a need. Before we know where we are, we are doing all kind of good works, but not afore prepared that we should walk in them. Therefore, they do not go into the kingdom. That is why this has to be a way of faith. "This is the victory that overcometh the world, even our faith."

> *Work out your own salvation with fear and trembling; for it is God who worketh in you both to will and to work, for his good pleasure. (Philippians 2:12b,13)*

Now isn't that an extraordinary statement? It is Armenian and Calvinist in one sentence. Keep in Christ. Keep in union with Christ and you can work out your salvation practically. Make it yours, appropriate it, experience it, enter into it. Then you will find that as you stay in union with Christ, it is God who is in you working both to will and to work of His good pleasure.

A LIFE LAID DOWN

> *I am the good shepherd: the good shepherd layeth down his life for the sheep. (John 10:11)*

> *Therefore doth the Father love me, because I lay down my life, that I may take it again. No one taketh it away from me, but I lay it down of myself. I have power to lay it down, and I have power to take it again. This commandment received I from my Father. (verses 17-18)*

> *Have this mind in you, which was also in Christ Jesus: who, existing in the form of God, counted not the being on an equality with God a thing to be grasped, but emptied himself, taking the form of a servant, being made in the likeness of men; and being found in fashion as a man, he humbled himself, becoming obedient*

even unto death, yea, the death of the cross. Wherefore also God highly exalted him, and gave unto him the name which is above every name; that in the name of Jesus every knee should bow, of things in heaven and things on earth and things under the earth, and that every tongue should confess that Jesus Christ is Lord, to the glory of God the Father. (Philippians 2:5-11)

That was the secret of the Lord Jesus' overcoming, and we see it not just in Calvary. You make a great mistake if you think the only time Jesus laid down His life was at Calvary. That was the supreme expression of it as if the whole matter was condensed finally in that one supreme sacrifice of Himself for our sins, but Bethlehem was the beginning. Somewhere in eternity, before times eternal, when the Father said, "Whom shall I send and who will go for Us?" the Son said, "Here am I, send Me."

Then said I, Lo, I am come; In the roll of the book it is written of me: I delight to do thy will, O my God; Yea, thy law is within my heart. (Psalm 40:7-8)

Bethlehem was the beginning of it. There would have been no incarnation unless the Lord Jesus had laid down His life. We find it in one of our lovely hymns by Wesley, "He laid His glory by; He emptied Himself of all but love."

We have it again in the River Jordan. When Jesus came to the River Jordan, I do not believe there was a single encouragement from heaven for Him. God left Him to Himself so that He could face that whole issue. After thirty years of life in which He had not sinned, in which He had been perfectly holy, in which He had met all kinds of problems and trials and overcame them, He came to the last three years. These three years of His public ministry were going to end in the sacrifice of Himself on the cross. Those waters of baptism were not because Jesus needed to wash away sins. They were not because He just wanted to give us an example that we should be baptized. Of course it was an example, but that is a very weak thing if that is the only reason for it.

Why did Jesus get baptized? He said it was to fulfill all righteousness. Those waters of baptism symbolized the death of the cross. Three years before Jesus ever came to the death of the cross He said, "Father, I am ready to go to the cross." He laid down His life again, and in that moment that He laid down His life, the heavens opened and God said, "This is My beloved Son in whom I am well pleased." The Holy Spirit came down in the form of a dove and settled upon Him.

John the Baptist had said that He whom he saw the Holy Spirit coming upon would be the Messiah. There is no doubt in my mind that when John the Baptist saw the dove, he immediately knew. Some people say that the dove was a symbol of the mildness of the Holy Spirit, the meekness of the Holy Spirit, the gentleness of Christ, the humility of Christ. I know doves are symbols of that, but to me that is not the symbolism. If you were a rich person you brought a bullock for your sin offering, if you were middle class you brought a ram, but if you belonged to the vast working class, the peasants of the land of whom the great majority belonged, you brought two turtle doves. The moment John the Baptist saw the Holy Spirit coming down as a dove he said, "That is it, the sacrifice. Behold the Lamb of God who beareth away the sin of the world." The Holy Spirit was coming upon Jesus to enable Him to lay down His life every day for three years and, finally, in a supreme sacrifice for sin.

When you come to the transfiguration, you have the same thing again. When Jesus was transfigured in glory, it was not as a spotlight of glory from heaven. That is how we often imagine it, with Jesus and the two disciples standing there and suddenly a spotlight of glory came down from heaven and shone upon Him, all around Him. It does not say that. It says that something was switched on inside of Him so that His whole flesh was transfigured, so that His clothes glistened, as no bleacher could ever make them white. It was a glory that came from inside of Him. The first Adam fell short of the glory of God, but the last Adam came into the glory of God. At that point, Jesus could have stepped onto the throne, into the kingdom and said, "Father, I claim it." But He turned around, went down, and in a week or two, He was dead. That is why the voice of God was heard, "Behold, this is My beloved Son, hear ye Him."

Gethsemane was the same thing again. Every pressure in hell came upon Jesus in that moment so that He sweat great drops as of blood. This means that the most tremendous mental and emotional pressure was put upon the Lord Jesus. We do not know the hideous and horrifying visions and pictures, apparitions that the devil brought before the Lord Jesus. I have no doubt that it was to do with the cost of our salvation, as if the devil were saying, "Once You die, it will be permanent. What guarantee do You have that once You have borne sin, once You have taken it upon Yourself, that You will not be cast off forever, alienated forever."

We do not know exactly what it was that came before the Lord Jesus, but we know that an angel had to strengthen Him before the most terrible part of the ordeal, not at the end of it. An angel came from heaven and strengthened Him and ministered to Him, so He could go through it. The whole battle was won with these words, "Not as I will, but as Thou wilt."

And Jesus was the only one who had peace. When Judas came with that great armed rabble plus the temple guards, everyone of them panicked, but not Jesus. When Peter took a sword and cut off the high priest's servant's ear, Jesus touched it and healed him and said, "Do not do that."

Then, of course, He went to Calvary. When Jesus went down into death, God exalted Him far above all. "Wherefore also God hath highly exalted Him and given Him that name which is above every name." If we would come to the throne, then we must also lay down our lives. There is no other way to overcome. Do not think that you can come to the throne by holding onto your life. If you think you can, you are in danger of deception. If you hold onto your life, it will effectively divorce you from the throne of Christ. You will not lose your salvation, but you will not come to the throne.

Hereby know we love, because he laid down his life for us: and we ought to lay down our lives for the brethren. (I John 3:16)

There is no compulsion in this matter. "We ought also to lay down our lives." God does not want people on the throne because they have to be there. If you think God wants Christians all draped around on thrones throughout the universe because they really did not want to get there, but finally they got there, you are mistaken. The Lord Jesus said that He would do the will of the Father, "I delight to do Thy will," and so came into this world. So, you and I have to, of our own will, will to do the will of God. God will never push anyone into this matter of coming to the throne. The principle is that we lose our lives to find our lives. Do not forget it.

Have you found your life? Many Christians come to me and say, "I know something is missing." They have not found their life. They have plenty of experiences. They rush off here and there and get this and get that, and it is good, but there is always something missing. You will never find your life unto life eternal unless you lose it. We die that we might know the power of His resurrection. There is no other way. Do you want to know the power of His resurrection? Then you must die. We fall into the ground and die that there might be a harvest. There is no other way. We humble ourselves and God exalts us. We make ourselves of no reputation and God gives us an eternally known name.

I could give you example after example of that. John Wesley's name will remain to the end of eternity, but in his day he was the offscouring. George Fox's name will be alive as long as there is the kingdom of God, but he was the offscouring in his day. You make yourself of no reputation and God will give you an eternally known name. We are broken that others might be blessed. We deny ourselves and discover the fulness of God. We take up the cross and He brings us to the throne of His glory. Until we are prepared to lay down our lives, we never know the real nature of our old man, of our talents, of our gifts, of our personality.

It is an amazing thing that after that tremendous encounter with God, Moses said, "If I go, Lord, will they really believe me?"

God said, "What is that in your hand?"

Moses said, "It is a rod," and God said, "Throw it down."

When he threw it down, it became a poisonous viper. Then God said to him, "Take it up by the tail."

Now anyone who knows anything about snakes, knows that you never, never take up a viper by its tail. You always take it up just behind the head. Moses had spent forty years in the desert, and he knew very well it was the stupidest, silliest thing that could ever have been said to him. If you take a poisonous viper up by the tail it curls, and then stings you.

There was no Red Cross out there to rush to him and give him an antidote. He knew very well he would die a painful, unhappy death, within moments.

What was God doing? That rod was the rod of authority. That was the rod that Moses was to lift up and the sea was to part into two. That was the rod that he was to touch the rock and water flowed out of it. That was the rod again and again that God used. How then could it have been a poisonous viper? Only when he let it go did he find the poison of a self-life in it.

Dear child of God, you are never safe until you have let go of any ministry you have or anything you have of any kind. When you hold onto it, you are not even aware that there is a poisonous viper lurking there, but when you throw it down, suddenly the truth becomes apparent. There is the poison of a self-life in it. Once you see what your motives are or what is interwoven with it you have such a bad time. Then God says, "Take it by the tail." You have got to take that viper by the tail in faith; then you have a rod of authority.

Then God said to Moses, "See your hand; put it in your bosom on your heart." When he took it out, it was leprous, as white as snow. Emotions, hand, action. We do not realize these things, do we? It is only when you lay down your life you are safe. You can be in full time service, you can have a real ministry, but until you have let go, you are not safe. The cross is the only way to the throne, to reigning with Christ.

THE MINISTRY OF THE HOLY SPIRIT

Christ was born of the Spirit; He was indwelt by the Spirit; He knew the fruit of the Spirit; He was anointed by the Spirit; He manifested the gifts of the Spirit; He fulfilled the work of our salvation by the power of the Spirit.

And the angel answered and said unto her, The Holy Spirit shall come upon thee, and the power of the Most High shall overshadow thee: wherefore also the holy thing which is begotten shall be called the Son of God. (Luke 1:35)

Now it came to pass, when all the people were bap-
tized, that, Jesus also having been baptized, and pray-
ing, the heaven was opened, and the Holy Spirit de-
scended in a bodily form, as a dove, upon him, and a
voice came out of heaven, Thou art my beloved Son: in
thee I am well pleased. (Luke 3:21-22)

And Jesus, full of the Holy Spirit, returned from the
Jordan, and was led in the Spirit in the wilderness.
(Luke 4:1)

For of a truth in this city against thy holy Servant Jesus,
whom thou didst anoint... (Acts 4:27a)

Even Jesus of Nazareth, how God anointed him with
the Holy Spirit and with power: who went about doing
good, and healing all that were oppressed of the devil;
for God was with him. (Acts 10:38)

When did God anoint Jesus? It was at His baptism that
Jesus was anointed. He was born of the Holy Spirit, He was
indwelt by the Holy Spirit, and then He was anointed by the
Holy Spirit.

How much more shall the blood of Christ, who
through the eternal Spirit offered himself without
blemish unto God, cleanse your conscience from dead
works to serve the living God? (Hebrews 9:14)

This is often explained that it was by the Spirit Jesus actually went to the cross. That is true. But have you ever noticed that He offered Himself up to God without spot or
blemish? In other words, He had gone through the whole of
those three years by the eternal Spirit, keeping Himself without spot or blemish so that He might in the end, by the same
Spirit, offer Himself up to God as a sacrifice for sin. If Christ
needed to know the gracious ministry of the Holy Spirit, how
much more we need to know it!

*But we received, not the spirit of the world, but the spirit
which is from God; that we might know the things that
were freely given to us of God. (I Corinthians 2:12)*

No one can know the fulness of Christ, the resources of
Christ, the unsearchable riches of Christ, in experience, apart
from the ministry of the Holy Spirit. That is why the word is:
be being filled with the Spirit. How else can we experience all
that is ours in Christ? How else can we know practically our
union with Christ? How can we do greater works than He did,
if He did it by the Holy Spirit? We must never forget that
overcoming is linked forever with the Holy Spirit.

When God spoke to Zechariah, He said, "Not by might,
nor by power but by My Spirit, saith the Lord of Hosts."
There is no other way to overcoming. There is no other way
to the throne. Isn't it interesting that Jesus spoke to the
church and said, "To him that overcometh. . . to him that
overcometh. . . to him that overcometh"? The vision we have
is that Jesus was in the midst of those seven golden lampstands. He was speaking, but He said, "He that hath an ear let
him hear what the *Spirit* saith to the churches."

I think this matter of the Holy Spirit is one of the most
important matters. There is excess, there is that which is artificial, there is that which is superficial, but believe me, there is
that which is absolutely real. Woe betide any child of God
who does not know the gracious ministry of the Holy Spirit in
all His fulness, His indwelling, His empowering, being born of
the Spirit, the anointing of the Spirit, the fruit of the Spirit, the
baptism of the Spirit, and the gifts of the Spirit. You will
never be transformed into the same image from glory to glory
unless it is by the Lord, the Spirit.

PERFECTED THROUGH SUFFERINGS

We have said that union with the Father, a life laid down,
and the ministry of the Holy Spirit were keys to Christ's overcoming. The fourth thing is that He was perfected through
sufferings. It is amazing to consider that Christ, though sinless, was yet made perfect through suffering. The word
means: *complete, full, ended.* We sometimes translate it *full-
grown.* This Greek word can be translated in different ways

but the idea is not just moral perfection, as we often think, but really something complete, fully rounded, full-grown. The way of Christ to the Father's throne was through suffering.

Though he was a Son, yet learned obedience by the things which he suffered; and having been made perfect, he became unto all them that obey him the author of eternal salvation. (Hebrews 5:8-9)

Think for a moment. This was Jesus. He learned obedience by the things which He suffered. The character of His service, of His kingship, was made full, was completed, was filled out by suffering, by learning obedience. He learned the full meaning and nature of obedience through the things which He suffered.

My dear child of God, you will never ever learn the full meaning and nature of obedience except through the things which you suffer. The kingship of Christ is not based on His pedigree, although He has a pedigree, nor even on His divinely given status or title; He was born King of the Jews. It is based on the royalty of His character in His humiliation at His trial. There, He was divested of all the mystique of royalty, that kind of distance royalty keep, that regalia, that pomp, the kind of difference between royalty and ordinary mortals. When Jesus was divested of all that, stripped naked, so that He looked just like any other man, when He was beaten, disfigured, derided, spat upon, then we see His real nature. When all the things that make up that kind of dignity that most men would lose at such a time had gone, then we see in Christ a majesty, an authority, a royalty, a nobility, which is not based upon outward trappings and position, but on inward character. Such a one must reign. He makes the crown of thorns the most glorious crown ever worn in the history of this world. He makes that reed the most powerful scepter ever wielded in human history.

With God, kingship cannot be just a matter of status, of title and pedigree as if God is out for a kind of heavenly bureaucracy. It must be also a matter of character and experience. If this is so even of Christ, how much more of us? Just because we are born again, just because we are saved by the grace of God, does not mean that we have the ability to reign.

The universe in the ages to come will be in a sorry mess if it is left to some Christians to supervise it, to have dominion over it and administer it. No, we can only reign if we are prepared for suffering and discipline. That is why it says, "If we endure, we shall also reign with Him, if we suffer with Him, we shall also be glorified with Him." That is why we have the "if" in so many of these verses in connection with the kingdom, with kingship.

Thus, our routine life and circumstances become the school in which God trains us for kingship—the home, the kitchen sink, the office, the factory bench. (Trials and troubles come to all human beings, and some who are unsaved take them better than some who are saved.) The inexplicable trials given to those marked out for kingship all become the means for our being perfected.

This matter of perfection is used so much in the New Testament: "That you might come to a perfect man." "That He might present everyone of you perfect."

We have got to learn the real nature and meaning of obedience by the things we suffer. It is not merely negative but positive. An understanding, a compassion, a sensitivity comes this way only. Someone who has known discipline, someone who has known suffering, someone who has gone through the mill, has a deep fund of compassion and understanding in their administering of the will of God. You cannot get that by an idealistic, theoretical training. It has to come through learning obedience by the things which we suffer. Learning obedience is the key to being perfected, being full-grown, being completed. The Father brought the Son to the throne this way. Now, with amazing and incredible grace He works on the poor material that we all are. If we will only let Him, He will take us through discipline and suffering to His throne, there to reign forever.

The Lion of Judah is also, at the same time, the little Lamb as it had been slain in the midst of the throne. That is God's idea and concept of kingship and authority. The Lion is majestic power and authority, but the Lion is the little Lamb as it had been slain. None of us can sit down in the Lamb's throne if we have not become like the Lamb. May the Lord work this into us all that we may overcome as our Lord Jesus has overcome.

THREE SPHERES OF REIGNING
WITH CHRIST

Revelation 1:12-20—And I turned to see the voice that spake with me. And having turned I saw seven golden candlesticks; and in the midst of the candlesticks one like unto a son of man. (verses 12-13a)

Revelation 2:7,11,17,26-29—He that hath an ear, let him hear what the Spirit saith to the churches. To him that overcometh, to him will I give to eat of the tree of life, which is in the Paradise of God.

He that hath an ear, let him hear what the Spirit saith to the churches. He that overcometh shall not be hurt of the second death. He that hath an ear, let him hear what the Spirit saith to the churches. To him that overcometh, to him will I give of the hidden manna, and I will give him a white stone, and upon the stone a new name written, which no one knoweth but he that receiveth it.

And he that overcometh, and he that keepeth my works unto the end, to him will I give authority over the nations: and he shall rule them with a rod of iron, as the vessels of the potter are broken to shivers; as I also have received of my Father: and I will give him the morning star. He that hath an ear, let him hear what the Spirit saith to the churches.

Revelation 3:5,6,12,13,21,22—He that overcometh shall thus be arrayed in white garments; and I will in no wise blot his name out of the book of life, and I will confess his name before my Father, and before his angels. He that hath an ear, let him hear what the Spirit saith to the churches. He that overcometh, I will make him a pillar in the temple of my God, and he shall go out thence no more: and I will write upon him the name of my God, and the name of the city of my God,

*the new Jerusalem, which cometh down out of heaven
from my God, and mine own new name. He that hath
an ear, let him hear what the Spirit saith to the
churches. He that overcometh, I will give to him to sit
down with me in my throne, as I also overcame, and
sat down with my Father in his throne. He that hath
an ear, let him hear what the Spirit saith to the
churches.*

*Revelation 21:5-7—And he that sitteth on the throne
said, Behold, I make all things new. And he saith,
Write: for these words are faithful and true. And he
said unto me, They are come to pass. I am the Alpha
and the Omega, the beginning and the end. I will give
unto him that is athirst of the fountain of the water of
life freely. He that overcometh shall inherit these
things; and I will be his God, and he shall be my son.*

I would like to look at this matter of reigning with Christ
or overcoming in three very practical, vital spheres in which
the Lord is looking for us to reign with His Son here and now.
If we are going to know something of reigning with Him in the
kingdom that is to come, really sitting down with Him in His
throne and administering the government of God in the ages
that are to come, there are three spheres in which we, as the
people of God, have got to know overcoming.

It is very interesting to look at the book of Revelation. It
has had many complex theories developed upon it. When one
reads some of the books on it, one almost feels like putting an
ice pack on one's head and going back to the Bible for relief.
On the whole, we find the things written on the book of
Revelation to be extremely hard to take in. Of course, if you
confine yourself to only one book you will do a little better.
But if you are an avid reader and start off on one book, you
may feel like you have some sort of pattern or outline for the
book of Revelation. Then you read another which completely
demolishes the first and that is when you begin to get somewhat confused and perplexed. If you go on to the third and
fourth and fifth, they tend to demolish all the previous theories. In the end, you sink almost for the third time, never to

come up again on the matter of a clear understanding of the book of Revelation.

It is an interesting fact that the book of Revelation was one of the books most contested in the early church. In fact, it did not come to its final position as the last book of the canon of Scripture until about the fourth century after Christ. Then it was finally, universally recognized and accepted and came to occupy the last place in the sixty-six books of the Bible. Of course, it was the sovereignty of God that brought this book to its right place as the conclusion of inspired Scripture, as the summing up of the Word of God. It is therefore very interesting that when we come to it we find that there is so much to do with the overcomer.

The book opens with the risen Christ in the midst of seven very ordinary local churches. A number of the other churches that we have records of in Acts are not mentioned here, but seven are selected. We find an extraordinary vision of the risen Christ in the midst of seven golden lampstands, each of which represents one of these local churches. Our Lord could have said all kinds of things to these churches; but, without exception, after putting His finger upon anything that was wrong in those churches or finding nothing wrong, commending them, He ends up His message to each of the seven churches by speaking about the overcomer. Therefore, we can only deduce that this matter of overcoming is of tremendous importance to our risen Lord. If He had not mentioned it with Philadelphia, it would have perhaps lessened it a little, but to the church at Philadelphia He says even more about overcoming. Some of the most glorious things said about overcoming are said to the church which He commends. Our Lord looks at the churches, that is, the church in time and on earth and in given localities. Whether He sees right or wrong, whether He can only commend or only rebuke, whether it is a mixture of rebuke and commendation, the one message that comes through, that sums up everything that is on His heart, is the matter of overcoming. Today, our Lord is still in the midst of churches, still speaking, still removing lampstands, still rebuking, still commending, and still saying the same thing about overcoming. Two thousand years have made no difference to the vital importance of this matter to our Lord because this whole matter of overcoming is to do with the ages to come. It is to do with the administration of the kingdom; it is to do with the throne of God and its practical outworking.

It is interesting that when we come to the end of the book of Revelation, we find no more talk about local churches, no more talk about the people of God on earth, in time, on earth and in given localities. Instead, we find the holy city, the new Jerusalem, the wife of the Lamb, the bride of Christ coming down out of heaven having the glory of God. In Revelation 21:6,7 we have an extraordinary bringing together of two things: "I will give unto him that is athirst of the fountain of the water of life freely." This seems to speak about salvation and almost initial things in the Christian life. Then our Lord goes on to this matter which is the objective of everything: "He that overcometh shall inherit these things; and I will be his God, and he shall be my son." In other words, this is a marvelous picture of a grown-up son; a son who can take responsibility, a son who can administer the will of his Father and the riches of his Father and the power and authority of his Father.

We saw at the beginning seven golden lampstands. When we come to the end of the book of Revelation, we have really *one* great golden lampstand. We are told that the light in which the nations will walk will be the glory of God and of the Lamb. "The glory of God did lighten it and the Lamb is the lamp thereof." Then who is the stand? The lampstand is the city. The lampstand, you and I, those who, by the grace of God alone have overcome, constitute the lampstand. The Lamb is the lamp and the glory of God is the light in the lamp.

> *And there shall be no curse any more: and the throne of God and of the Lamb shall be therein: and his servants shall serve him; and they shall see his face; and his name shall be on their foreheads. And there shall be night no more; and they need no light of lamp, neither light of sun; for the Lord God shall give them light: and they shall reign for ever and ever.* (Revelation 22:3-5)

It is a most wonderful word, profound in its simplicity; but, tremendous in its power. In the midst of it all we have this word in Revelation 12:11:

And they overcame him because of the blood of the Lamb, and because of the word of their testimony; and they loved not their life even unto death.

In this last book of the Bible, this conclusion of the inspired canon, we have an overall picture beginning with the risen Christ in the midst of the seven golden lampstands. We see Him speaking to saints, believers, redeemed children of God, meeting together in a special way on a certain foundation, about this matter of overcoming. Then we span the whole age, and we see at the end the golden lampstand itself. The glory of God is the light; the Lamb is the lamp; the stand is the city, and we see the nations walking in the light of it. We hear again those wonderful words as that wife of the Lamb comes down out of heaven, "He that overcometh shall inherit these things and I will be his God and he shall be my son."

INDIVIDUAL LIFE

One of the spheres in this matter of kingship, or overcoming is related to the individual. You cannot hide in the mass. There is something about us all that likes to hide in the mass. We are always talking about the heaviness of the whole thing and how difficult it is, but we hide in the mass. We would hate it if we were suddenly put on the spot. We would hate it if suddenly some divine finger were to isolate us and say, "Now you!" We love to be able to talk about the whole and say, "Oh, it is so difficult; they are this and they are that." But we do not want to be isolated. We would die a million deaths if the finger of the Spirit were to point to us and we were isolated and challenged, and then we really had to do something.

We live in the days of mass media, mass movements, everything is *en masse*. We have never had a population problem such as we have today. It is a very easy thing for believers now, having seen something of the nature of the church, having seen something of the essential corporate nature of what God is doing, to hide in the mass. You only have to have a nucleus of people who really know the Lord and know what God is after, and the rest can hide in it. Until they are taken to be with the Lord, or something happens, they can hide. We can just drift along in a fool's paradise thinking we are really getting places when, in fact, God says we are getting nowhere. We come along to times of worship, or to times of prayer, never really participating, but comforting ourselves that somehow or other our very presence surely is some sign to God. We seem to think that God looks on the heart (which He certainly does) and does not take too much note of the lip. We are entirely wrong. You are not only saved with the heart, but with the lip, and that is a principle that we find shot through everything. It is not until we are prepared to confess with the lip what we believe in the heart that God commits Himself fully.

One of the great problems of a second generation is hiding in the mass. May the Lord preserve us from a second generation. May we all be first generation in spirit. A second generation finds that everything has been done by the first generation. The essential battles have been fought and won, all the positions have been spied out and taken, and then the second generation comes into all the good of it. It is very possible to hide in the first generation, just to come along into it without original, personal, intimate, direct experience of the Lord.

With all our Lord's concern for the building of the church, for all our Lord's avowed concern for the completion of the house of God, not on a single occasion does He say, "To *those* who have an ear to hear, let *them* hear what the Spirit says." Normally you would think if God was speaking to the church He would say, "Let *them* hear." But the Lord does not say that. He says, "*He* that hath an ear, let *him* hear." The whole accent and emphasis is upon the individual. You cannot escape. You cannot blame the elders, you cannot blame other responsible brothers or sisters, you cannot blame the company of believers you are in. It is a corporate matter, but it is a question of *your* ear, *your* hearing, *your* attending, *your* understanding, *your* obedience.

In some cases it is extraordinary the way the Lord emphasizes the thing, as in Revelation 2:7 where He says it twice: *He that hath an ear, let him hear what the Spirit saith to the churches. To him that overcometh, to him will I give to eat of the tree of life, which is in the Paradise of God.* (See also Revelation 2:11,17,26 and 3:5,12,21.)

The Lord puts His finger on personal, original, spiritual character. You will never get that secondhand. You may find a little bit of other people's character brush off on you; you may find something of their experience brush off on you, but there is one thing you can never get and that is secondhand experience. It is only really hearsay. You have to have your *own* experience of the Lord, your *own* experience of coming to a place of ascendancy, your *own* experience of being made to sit together with Christ in heavenly places. Where is it going to happen? It has to first of all happen within your personal circumstances. That is why so often our Lord takes very real note of the very small things in our lives. If we cannot get the ascendancy at the kitchen sink, we are certainly not going to reign with Christ in the ages to come. If we cannot get ascendancy in the office, we are not going to have ascendancy in the ages to come. We sometimes think, "Oh, these little things;" but, it is these little things that make or break us. It is in these very small petty circumstances, the routine of daily life that somehow or other this whole matter of overcoming is reduced to a question of spiritual character, your spiritual character, my spiritual character.

Someone may have faith to remove a mountain, to tackle a big problem. Thank God, *they* use it and see that obstacle disappear. Of course you are full of joy. You may come in on the good of it, but it has not done anything for *you*. Even though you come into blessing, you come into some spiritual facility because of it, you have not been made one whit more able to govern.

What I am trying to say is that you will not always have great big problems, such as the church has to face at times, but God will allow a lot of problems to come into your life so that *you* have to face them in faith or unbelief. There is no alternative. You can face it in unbelief and say, "No, no, it cannot happen, not to me; I am such a small person, such an insignificant person. Of course, I suppose the Lord is angry with me anyway." You do not know what it is to have the faith of Abraham. There are issues in your life where God speaks to you and only *you* can have the obedience of faith. I cannot do it for you, neither can you do it for me. We can bless one another. Thank God for the blessing. It is a dreadful thing to be a curse to one another or a weight on one another. What a wonderful thing it is when we are a blessing to the saints, just our presence, just our contribution, just our experience is a blessing to others. People feel it as they come to us; they touch us. You may be the greatest blessing in the whole world to me and to everybody else, but unless *I* learn to exercise faith, unless *I* know resurrection life as we saw it in Isaac, unless *I* know what it is to be transformed by the renewing of my mind personally, unless *I* know what it is to come to the throne through discipline and suffering, there is no possibility of real advance in *my* life in this matter of overcoming.

Our Lord Jesus learned obedience by the things He suffered. *You* cannot learn obedience by *my* obedience. You and I will only learn obedience through the things which each one of us suffer. God is so kind and loving. He does not give you the kind of things He gave Watchman Nee. If God were to allow you to get brainwashed, it is not only your brain that would get washed, you would probably disappear. God is so gracious in these things. We say, "Oh, I would never. . ." Of course you could not. God does not put you in prison in solitary confinement for twenty years. He knows it would just finish you, but God has given you your own little experience of trial.

God has allowed to come into your circumstances the kind of things which, in His loving grace and mercy, are absolutely suitable to you. Now, you may not think so. The devil comes and says, "You cannot worship the Lord. If you got this thing removed you could, but how can you overcome with a boss like that? It would ruin anyone's life. Your family circumstances are bad and with children like that? If you were like so and so, with that marvelous pattern family, you would be raring to go, but you just cannot do it. And remember what it says in Timothy."

So we sink into ourselves; we are finished. We feel that our circumstances are really almost too much, and if the Lord does not change them it is the end. In actual fact, God knows all about your circumstances. They have been allowed with a very real wisdom behind them because they are just what is required for you to grow up in Christ. He does not give you the big things. He gives you what you can bear, but you do not feel that you can bear them.

Now, supposing the Lord gives you something that you can just walk over. "Ah, now I can get my teeth into that, Lord." But that is not overcoming. If you can just walk over those things, that is not overcoming.

If the Lord gives you something and your immediate reaction is, "Oh, it is too much; that is finishing me," then it is either faith or unbelief. It is either resurrection life or death. It is either being transformed by the renewing of your mind, or your mind being fashioned according to this world. You either reject the discipline and suffering and do not come to the throne, or you accept it. God does not just carry us through. He allows things to come up which He knows very well are not too much for us. There is enough grace, there is enough spiritual character, there is enough faith in us to come through.

If we would only listen to the Lord on these things instead of listening to the enemy, it would change our whole attitude to our personal circumstances, to problems we are facing. We would see it as a tremendous challenge to the Lord in us. "My Father is behind this. Even if it is a messenger from Satan, my Father is behind this thing and He has a purpose of GRACE in all this to draw out in me the character and life of His Son."

Now, you may go down. Do not be frightened of going down. People seem to think they should never go down, that in the Christian life you are always above, but that is not the principle of Calvary. You must go down in order to come up, and the more you go down, the more you will come up. It is an unalterable law. It is a very hard thing when you are going down to say, "Aha! Well, praise God, I am going down because I am going to go up." But once you have really seen the Lord work in this way, you can almost rejoice as you are on the way down. If you go down farther than you have ever gone down before, well, praise the Lord, you will go up farther than you have ever been before. It is an unalterable law. If you go down, you must go up, *providing* there is faith.

If you go down with unbelief and all that false artificial modesty that so many of us dress ourselves up with, of course you do not emerge. You go down to the bottom and stay on the bottom. You have to go down in faith; you are letting go. You are not letting go of God's purpose for you to bring you to the throne. You are not letting go of the fact that you are going to be above and not beneath, that you are going to be the head and not the tail, that you should be set up on high, that you should be made to sit together with Christ in heavenly places. But you know that the way to go up is to go down. It is a matter of letting go and surrendering. You allow the breaking. Thus you see God works in the most wonderful way in our personal circumstances, in our business life, in our family life. This is where God puts the whole thing to the test. "To him that overcometh, to him will I grant this and this and this."

There can be no coming to the throne *en masse*. Thank God for fellowship, thank God for being able to share, thank God for the prayer of the church, but you and I will never come to the throne just simply because of others. We will only ever come to the throne because of the Lord in us, each one.

I think it is a salutary thing to remind ourselves that we have finite minds, created minds, that are incapable, ever, of holding the whole truth. Not even at the end of eternity will one person hold the whole truth. One of our problems is that when we get a new truth, we expel an old one. We just cannot hold the new truth along with the old. We are not like the man whom our Lord said had old treasures as well as new ones. We get rid of the old treasures, and we can only trade in the new. That is a mistake. We have very small minds.

I think it is a tremendous thing just to remember that God has a purpose for every one of our lives and that He has chosen our circumstances and our way for us because He has a way to bring us to the throne. Now, I trust the Lord will forgive me for saying this, but He knows what I mean. You see, if I had been the Lord, I would never have allowed Watchman Nee to be in prison for twenty years. The whole world is crying out for ministry, for real ministry of the Word, for deep ministry of the Word, for vision of God's purpose, and here is a vessel that has not only seen, but has been tested to the nth degree. I would have said, "We will put him in for five years, ten years, fifteen years, even twenty years; but, then we will get him out and send him all over the world. We will let people see what I have done in this man. We will let people taste of what I have done in this man. We will let this man become a chosen vessel, by which all of this is poured out in even greater force than ever before." Not God. He takes a man with one of the greatest ministries in the history of the church, and He shuts him up in a solitary cell for twenty years. When he is released, within a month he dies. Now the world would say, "That is waste." But you will discover one day that God had such a concern for men, for His government, that He was prepared to take a man with a ministry like that and put him in a cell for twenty years in order to teach him to reign with Christ.

That may explain a lot of things that God is doing with you on a very much smaller level and scale. We think we are so clever; we even question God. We argue with God. We tell Him, the potter, "What do you think you are doing? You should not do it like this. You should do it this way." But God knows exactly what He is doing. This matter of reigning with Christ is so important, that He will even take a man like that, who knew more about the body of Christ than probably anyone else, at least who was able to communicate truth about it in a most wonderful and living way, and train him alone.

God did the same with the apostle Paul. I know he called himself, Paul the aged, but he was only sixty-six. We do not think of someone sixty-six as being aged, but God took him home at sixty-six years of age. You would have thought the churches could have done with him for another ten years. Think of the letters that could have been written. Think of the counsel. Perhaps those churches that turned away from him in Asia could have been somehow strengthened. Perhaps some of the rot that began to set in could have been halted, maybe even purged out. But not the Lord. He evidently taught Paul things in those last days and years in prison that were entirely to do with the age to come, entirely to do with government.

I remember years ago listening to an old servant of the Lord give a testimony at Honor Oak. To this day I remember that old sister, one of the tallest ladies I have ever seen, white-haired, eagle-nosed. She was Swiss and doing pioneering work. She said one thing I have never forgotten: "I am where there is no house of God, where there are no other believers, but I have proved daily the fellowship of the body of Christ." She was alone, but she knew the fellowship of the body of Christ. She stood into her position in the house of God. That does not mean that all of us should now go away and isolate ourselves. We have one another. We have the privilege of fellowship, the luxury of it, and all the advantages of it. But isn't it amazing that God can take a person out there in the jungle, with no possibility of fellowship, and teach them on their own, deep, deep lessons about the body of Christ. I am sure God did that with Watchman Nee, and with the apostle Paul and with many others.

This whole matter of kingship therefore is related to the individual. I dwell upon this matter because so often it is forgotten, and I note that in some of these movements that are going off the rails, it is on this very line that the rot seems to start. Somehow the whole thing becomes *en masse*, just simply drifting with one another. Now, we do not mean by being individuals, by having original spiritual character that we become queer or eccentric or somehow individualists. We mean that each one of us has our own knowledge of the Lord. Each one of us has our own experience of the Lord. More than that, each one of us is being brought to the place where we are sitting with Christ in heavenly places in our own circumstances.

CHURCH LIFE

The second sphere in this matter of kingship and overcoming is related to the house of God, to the church of God. You notice that *THE* overcomer, the Lord Jesus, is in the midst of seven churches. Those seven churches indicate the completeness of the church, whether you look at it as being the whole of church history in seven phases, as some interpret it, or whether you look upon it as the whole church of God in time and on earth. However we look at it, it is completeness, and it is in the midst of the churches that we find *the* overcomer, the One who has overcome and has sat down in His Father's throne.

Kingship or overcoming is related to the purpose of God. You cannot ever expect to administer the will of God and the government of God if you have been blind to the purpose of God in your own generation. People get into such a state over this. They say, "Oh, this matter of the church, what about Martin Luther? He did not see it. What about John Wesley?

He did not see it. What about George Fox?" Just wait. Martin Luther served the counsel of God in his own genera- tion. He obeyed what God showed him. He was an over- comer; so was Zwingli, so was Calvin and others. They saw truth, and they obeyed what God showed them. God never expected them to do more than what He had shown them. In their day, it was a phase of recovery and they gave themselves to the Lord for what He was out to recover. As it is said of David that he served the counsel of God in his own genera- tion.

What is the counsel of God in our generation? What is the thing God is doing in *our* generation? What is the phase of recovery that is in *our* generation? If you and I want to really know something about kingship, then we have got to see not only what was the purpose of God and what He has done, but we have to see what He is doing now and commit our- selves to it lock, stock, and barrel.

Wherever you find them, the overcomers in every gen- eration are those who served the counsel of God in their own generation. If Abraham had tried to be Enoch, he would have been a fool, and if Moses had tried to be Abraham, he would have been a fool. Supposing Moses had just gone out with his own family and said, "We will go to the Promise Land." No, he had to lead a people. Supposing Abraham had tried to take the whole of Ur. What if he had gone preaching in the streets of Ur and said, "Now everybody, if anyone here in Ur will come with me, God is going to make of me a great peo- ple."

No, God said to Abraham, "Get thee out of Ur of the Chaldees, out of thy father's house, out of thy kindred. You shall leave them." But when God spoke to Moses, He said, "You shall bring My people out of Egypt." Supposing Moses had said, "Now just wait. You took Abraham out on his own, so obviously there is some truth in this matter. I should leave father and mother. I will take Zipporah with me, but I will go alone." I am sure he would have shed a load of trouble, but he would never have come to the throne. He would never have been an overcomer.

In the day of the exile, the overcomers were the group that were with Zerubbabel and Ezra and Nehemiah. It was not Esther's lot, though thank God they knew deliverance and they knew blessing. They knew much else, and God was behind Esther marrying that heathen king, but I am sorry to say they were not related vitally to the purpose of God. But if we had lived in the days of the exile, and had argued that God had most wonderfully delivered us all in the exile, and we had a purity of worship, a purity of Bible study, a purity of fellowship, and the Lord was blessing us, we would have been entirely wrong. We need an understanding of the times we live in. I think this is a tremendously important matter.

Our Lord is in the midst of seven churches and they represent the whole church of God in time and on earth. There are also seven lampstands, and although our Lord said the seven lampstands are churches, it is perfectly clear that when He removed the lampstand the church went on. What then did our Lord mean with the lampstand, unless He meant the testimony of Jesus? In other words, this testimony of Jesus, which is the spirit of prophecy, is the thing that has been present at the beginning of every move of the Spirit of God in church history. If only people had ears to hear, they could have heard what the Spirit was saying to the churches at that time and would have heard the words of our Lord: "To him that overcometh will I grant to sit down with me in my throne, even as I also overcame, and sat down with my Father in his throne" (Revelation 3:22).

You see, as Christians we are so often living in the past. Only what is a hundred years old is respectable. Oh, for a spirit that is related to the purpose of God! Oh, for a heart that is devoted to what God is seeking to do in our own day and generation! Our generation is in a phase of recovery.

Notice the unhappy conditions in these churches, the Jezebels, Balaams, Nicolaitans, but it is interesting that our Lord never tells anyone to come out. Now these are not churches that we call churches. We make a great mistake when we think that these churches are what we see everywhere as churches. These were *real* churches. These were believers gathering together on the foundation of Jesus Christ alone, but there was much that was wrong. Whilst the lampstand was there the Lord never said, "Come out." In other words, we must always stay until the lampstand goes.

How do you know when the lampstand is gone? That is another matter, a very involved matter indeed. I have had to wrestle with this with some of our beloved brothers and sisters in things that are really going off the rails and they feel like the old exclusives, that if they come out it will be spiritual suicide. Indeed, many do have nervous breakdowns and much else because of this psychological bondage. Dear child of God, you and I are to stay with the lampstand. When the lampstand goes, we go. I shall be the first. Once the lampstand goes I would not stay a moment.

I remember that wonderful old lady that came to us, who was a prayer partner in the Billy Graham work. She had been a Methodist for many years, forgive me, any Methodists. She told me that for years she labored on while the ministry became more and more liberal and more and more unbelieving and the fellowship more and more social. But she said, "I had a loyalty to the whole thing and I felt that I must stay."

When the Lord showed her something and she got out, people came to her and said, "Miss So and so, how can you leave the sinking ship?"

And she said, "When I saw the captain get in the lifeboat, I knew it was time for me to leave."

I have never forgotten it. Why stay with a ship that has gone down when the captain Himself is in the lifeboat? If our Lord has gone, we go with our Lord. That is what Watchman Nee meant when he once said, "When the ark of the Lord and the tabernacle get parted, always follow the ark of the Lord."

We have to be careful here because in this subjective sphere we can deceive and delude ourselves. There may be issues or personal collisions and problems, and therefore it is a very easy thing to say, "The Lord is not with them. *I* am following the Lord."

How many times I have heard it and seen the tragic consequences and end of it all. I am simply trying to say here that though there may be very unhappy conditions in the life of these churches, our Lord tells us that we are to overcome there.

I have never failed to be amazed at this word in I Corinthians: "For there must be also factions among you, that they that are approved may be made manifest among you" (I Corinthians 11:19). I find this a remarkable way and it helps me to relax. If you are by nature a perfectionist, you like to rule out all those wrinkles and say, "There should not be anything." But the Word of God says, "There must be factions among you." There must be these problems, these warts, these blemishes, these things like boils in the body because this is the way the approved of God among you are made manifest. And they are not just made manifest to us, but to the unseen powers, the angels who are being instructed by what is happening in the church. Did you know you were an object lesson for unseen principalities and powers in which God is illustrating something and exhibiting something? It is very wonderful.

It seems to me that all that we are individually is put to the test here in this sphere of the house of God. If there is not anything there, we cannot get through, but if there is something there, we come through by the Lord in us. For instance, in the matter of fellowship and unity, we learn to give diligence to keep the unity of the Spirit in the bond of peace with all lowliness of mind. Very often it is a haughtiness of spirit and a haughtiness of mind that destroys the unity of the saints. We must have a lowliness of mind, giving diligence to keep the unity of the Spirit. You cannot keep the unity of the Spirit unless you know what your oneness is. If you think it is doctrine or details or technique or experiences, you are going to come unstuck, but if you know it is Christ, you know your foundation. The Holy Spirit is the custodian of the oneness of Christ, and He commits Himself to keeping that unity. It is a hard thing at times because, temperamentally, we are so different. I would say at least seventy-five percent of our problems in fellowship are due to temperamental collisions, a failure to recognize how the other party ticks. Oh, people get so upset about the person who is always ahead, who is always in the forefront, who is always taking the initiative, whose voice is always being heard. They say, "He must be empty because the deep ones keep their mouths sewn up."

Think about the apostle Paul who opened his mouth more than anybody else and in whom there was such depth. Yet, we have this idea that if a person is silent, silent waters run deep. We do not understand each other; we do not give time to recognize. Sometimes it is only after much experience that we do, and even then we do not understand this matter of the difference that there is in us all. Fellowship and unity is put to the test here.

How can we ever administer the government of God and the will of God if we have not known what it is to overcome in this simple matter of washing one another's feet? If we do not know what it is to love the brethren, to lay down our lives for one another, and not just for those we like, how can we possibly come to the throne of the One who gave Himself for all of us?

Contribution

Many of us keep our hearts closed, our minds shuttered and our lips jammed together when it comes to times of contribution. Yet, we are being built up a spiritual house to be a holy priesthood to offer up spiritual sacrifices acceptable to God through Jesus Christ (see I Peter 2:5).

Doesn't that disturb you? Now you may say, "There are too many of us on Sunday morning to contribute."

But even when you cut the number down to a quarter or a third the size, people still keep their mouths shut. There is no use saying, "He does not understand the problems."

I do understand the problems, but I cannot compromise on this matter of overcoming. Unless you learn to open your mouth and give what you have of the Lord, you will not come to the throne. Don't kid yourself and think that because it is all secret, you will still come to the throne. If you do not learn to communicate, you will never come to the throne because communication is one of the essential principles of kingship. Generally speaking, it is because of complexes, problems, inherited difficulties that we keep our mouth shut when it comes to really praising the Lord or contributing. If you have a talent and you are hiding it, you will be sure that talent will be taken away from you. But you say, "I put great value on it; I want the Lord to increase it. I have prayed about it."

Yes, but it is not only your heart the Lord wants, He wants your lips. If you are not prepared to share your Lord with the rest of the house of God, you cannot come to the throne.

There are many other scriptures on this matter about stirring up the gift that is within us, about giving ourselves to our particular ministry. But you say, "I do not know my ministry." One ministry you have is that you can pray. If you have never prayed before, begin now. Open your mouth and lead your brothers and sisters. Don't give one of those long flowery prayers. You must surely have a kindling of your heart when someone else is praying for something. Well, jump in. Do not wait for one of the big guns to get in. Just get in and say, "Lord, I second that." Then you can be quiet.

The enemy will come to you and say, "What a silly little thing for you to say. Such a small contribution. Do you think God has heard that?"

But the angels are absolutely joyous. "Listen to that; so and so came through tonight. It was just a few words, but it was wonderful!" Unless you learn to come in under the anointing and direction of the Holy Spirit, how can you come to the throne? It must have been very difficult to contribute in some of those companies mentioned, but there were overcomers.

Responsibility

Responsibility is bearing things upon our shoulders. How can anyone administer the government of God in the ages to come if they have not started to shoulder the responsibility down here? Maybe it is only small things, but that is just where we all begin.

Worship

What about the matter of worship? Many times I have heard people say, "Oh, I do not want to be part of those people who just use empty words." I have come to see that it is a disease amongst the people of God. Wherever one goes people say, "I do not want to open my mouth and be like the rest of them." They are keeping their treasures to themselves. Where did such pride come from? I would have thought that was the first thing that needed dealing with. Such a person must think he is the overcomer, but I do not call that overcoming. Our Lord is not like that. He stoops to hear the simplest cry and the most lisping praise. I know that there is sometimes empty praise. There are artificial phrases and all that dreadful preaching that I sometimes feel so sorry for our Lord over. No one has ever been more preached at than our Lord, when all He wants to hear is that He is loved and adored and appreciated. I sometimes think the Lord must be so hurt, but that is no excuse for *me* to shut up. If everyone else is going to be artificial, well by the grace of God, let me be real. Let me at least open my mouth and worship the Lord in spirit and in truth. But so often, these things we feel are phantoms; they are not even real. Sometimes we feel the people will not respond to anything we might give; then we find that everyone does.

Dear child of God, take these two things very much to heart. This matter of kingship is related to the individual, to our personal circumstances, to the producing of original, spiritual character, and it is also related to the house of God, to whatever phase in the purpose of God we happen to be in in our generation. It is also related to our life together in practical terms. Every time a person goes and washes someone's feet, that is, humbles himself before them and really loves them, it is the overcomer in him. It is the Lord. Every time a person gives diligence to keep the unity of the Spirit when there is every provocation to break it, it is the overcomer in him. Every time someone contributes something of the preciousness of Christ, when everything outside and around him would stop him, it is the overcomer in him. Every time you and I worship the Lord in spirit and in truth, it is the overcomer in us. May God make us a holy priesthood, offering up spiritual sacrifices. May our Lord see something of the travail of His own soul in us, in our attitude to one another, in our being built together, in the way we overcome the problems. No one will ever come to the throne unless God does it here. You may think God could do it for you in Australia or America or somewhere else, but God must do it here where we live, among the people we rub shoulders with. Even if we have a great ministry or no great ministry, here is the sphere in which you and I overcome among the people God has set us. May the Lord help us in this matter and may we hear those words afresh: "And now I vest in you the kingship which my Father vested in me."

AGAINST THE POWERS OF WORLD DARKNESS

The third sphere of kingship and overcoming is this matter of the house of God and the nations, or the house of God and the world, or the church and its testimony in the world. God's purpose for the body of Christ is not that they should just reign in the ages to come, but that they should reign *now,* and our job is to dislodge the powers of darkness from their usurped position in this world. Jesus said, "The prince of this world is cast out." Although we know that the apostle John said, "The world lieth in the evil one," yet it is our job to bring the kingdom of God to bear upon all kinds of situations. For instance, our Lord Jesus said, "Upon this rock I will build my church and the gates of hell shall not hold out against it, shall not prevail against it." Then He said in Matthew 16:19:

> *I will give unto thee the keys of the kingdom of heaven: and whatsoever thou shalt bind on earth shall be bound in heaven; and whatsoever thou shalt loose on earth shall be loosed in heaven.*

Let's think of it in another way: *keys of the kingship of heaven,* or *the authority of the throne.* Our Lord Jesus might have said, To thee I give the authority of my throne; I give you the authority that is in my name. Whatever you bind on earth shall be bound in heaven, and whatever you loose on earth shall be loosed in heaven. You will notice in your New American Standard Bible that it is put this way: "And whatever you shall bind on earth shall have been bound in heaven, and whatever you shall loose on earth shall have been loosed in heaven."

In other words, it is not that we say, "We think it would be a good idea if we did this and this and this. We think this should be released; we think that should be loosed and we do it in the name of Christ." It is done in a kind of magical way and we think that heaven has got to fall in with us. That is a mistaken idea among many dear people of God. That is where we can get uncovered, trying to push something through which is our own conception, according to our own view of things, and thinking therefore God has got to fall in with us. When it does not happen we become very disillusioned. We have to know what is the will of God and when, by the Spirit of the Lord, we get some real inner knowledge of the will of God, then we can carry it out. We know in our hearts that it is the will of God that this thing be bound. We have the go ahead in our hearts, and when that comes we can move forward in the name of the Lord Jesus. We can use the keys. Things can be bound. The church has suffered through its history because we have not learned to use the keys. At times we have not even known what it is to pray. But even when the people of God have known what it is to pray, they have not known what it is to *execute* the will of God, to take action by faith in the name of the Lord.

There are a whole number of ways in which this matter of overcoming is related to the world around us. It is related in the sense that there is material for the house of God which is as yet held fast by Satan. Only when those gates are unlocked, can those captives of the devil come out. Until you and I know what it is to reign with Christ, to be not beneath but above, to be not the tail but the head in Him, we cannot know that marvelous multiplication and increase that the early church knew.

One of the things I note again and again among the people of God is how almost unwittingly a heaviness may begin to develop. We can blame this on leadership, on ministry, on one another, but even when there was an Ananias and a Sapphira and many other things, the church, in the early days, did not stop growing or increasing. Of course, God dealt with it very strongly, but the fact is that those things do not stop the Lord going on, providing they are dealt with.

That heaviness, which is a weapon of the enemy, is like having a heavyweight wrestler sitting on top of you. "We wrestle not against flesh and blood but against principalities." A principality is not an evil spirit; he is rather weighty. We need to remember that when sometimes we find a principality or power. There is a great hierarchy of evil that is behind some of the things which can so delude and deceive people and can bind them for their whole life so they will not be open to anything more. Although we all believe this, we do not always recognize what is the outcome or the consequence of these things.

What is the consequence? There are times in our gatherings for prayer or in our times of worship, you find that something is sitting on everything. It is amazing how we can just sort of grit our teeth and go on, almost ignoring it. You cannot ignore a heavyweight wrestler sitting on you; otherwise you will lose. You have got to think how you can get out from under him and win. Now we have a tremendous advantage. Our Lord has already won, and the weapons of our warfare are not of the flesh, but are mighty before God to the pulling down of these strongholds. In other words, we can get right up from under these and through spiritual weapons and just by the declaration of eternal truth we can see the enemy defeated. But it really does need concerted action; you cannot do that alone. That is why we spoke about the individual, and about the house of God, but now we speak about the house of God and the nations, or the house of God and the world. In this kind of matter, we have got to be together. The Lord is teaching us vital lessons about kingship and overcoming just in these kinds of things.

Sometimes a heaviness can sit on a gathering until all of a sudden a number of people recognize it and rise up. Then everyone begins to be together, and the whole thing lifts in an instant. It is extraordinary! I have seen it again and again. Sometimes it is when the elders get together in prayer, or maybe the elders and workers get together in prayer, or maybe it is just the workers. Many, many times in our prayer times suddenly we have got hold of something, and sometimes weeks of heaviness are dispersed. Now that is reigning with Christ; that is overcoming.

You learn precious lessons there. For instance, one of the lessons you learn is that this world is an essentially spiritual world, that the things that are physical and material are really only, as it were, the concrete manifestation of spiritual realities.

Our Lord said concerning the Jewish people, "My Father's house shall be called a house of prayer for all nations, but you have made it a den of thieves," just a place of social intercourse, a place of formal and traditional religion, a place of commerce, of giving and receiving. That is what we can do with the house of God. We can prostitute it until it becomes nothing more than a social club, a lecture hall, a place where

we just have a certain amount of social intercourse. God preserve us from that for the Lord's purpose in the house of God
is that it might be a place in which the kingdom of God is
manifested and through it, an area, a locality, a nation, the
nations can be ruled.

It never fails to amaze me that a company of people can
seek the Lord in prayer on some national issue and see that
thing touched from heaven. One almost has an unbelief af-
terward that it could have possibly been prayer, that perhaps it
was going to happen anyway. But when we have seen some of
the remarkable things that have happened in our little history
as a result of prayer, one comes to the conclusion that we have
in our hands the most tremendous power in this world. We
have a power far greater than the Kremlin or Beijing exer-
cises. We have a power far greater than the White House or
Congress or our own Parliament has. We have a tremendous
power in our hands and we do not use it.

Dear child of God, if we do not use the power that has
been given to us in the name of Christ, if we do not use the
keys, we shall never come to the throne. In the eyes of the
Lord, it is the height of irresponsibility to have had something
provided through His grace and not use it. That is the severity
of the parable about the talents. Take it away from him and
give to him that has. It seems so unjust. Our whole order today, without getting political, is to take from him that has and
give it to him who has little. We must be very careful of poli-
tics in this matter, but I am stating a truth. Our whole phi-
losophy, even the most conservative, is to take from those that
have and give to those who do not have so much and thereby
level out. It seems therefore terribly undemocratic when we
hear the Lord saying not once, but on a number of occasions,
"Take away what he has and give to him that has." It seems
the exact opposite.

But what our Lord is saying is that these others have
learned to exercise responsibility. They have learned to rule
and to reign. They have learned in the school of experience
how to exploit things for the kingdom, how to exercise
authority. This man had the same possibilities. He was not
given five or two, but one. Nevertheless, he was given the
same provision of grace, the same provision of power. What
has he done with it? He has done nothing with it. He has not

learned how to exercise authority or how to reign and rule with Christ or how to bring the throne of God in on these things. He has not learned how to exploit things for the kingdom's sake. The only thing that person has done with his problems, his sufferings is to moan. That is all. Not that this one will lose his or her salvation; but, saved so as by fire. What was given for the kingdom, for the government, for the administration of the divine government in the ages to come, take it away from him and give it to the person who has learned. That may be the explanation of many a tear in the presence of the Lord, many a regret over wasted opportunities, over unexploited, unappropriated provision. It is not as if God has kicked you out into this world and said, "This is an evil place; it is now time for you to be kicked out into it and get on with it." God has given you armor, God has given you grace, God has given you power, God has given you every single thing you need to come to the throne.

This third sphere is vitally important. "If the salt has lost its savor, wherewith shall it be salted?" If the people of God are still the people of God, but have lost the power to reign, the power to rule in the unseen, the power to determine the course of things through the will of God, what other answer is there? Some people say to me, normally the most spiritual, "I do not see why we should be all bound up with praying for pornography or that kind of thing. There has always been pornography in the world. Our job is to go on with the Lord and grow in the Lord and see the house of God built." My dear friend, your attitude to evil in the town in which you live betrays your ability to reign with Christ. Your attitude to those very things which are wrecking and destroying other lives very much betrays the kind of spirit you have.

On the highest level, this matter of overcoming is therefore related to our secret place in union with the Head, really ruling and reigning over those things in our locality, in our nation, among the nations, and bringing to bear the kingdom of God upon them. I still believe that there are times when the people of God can be so industrious, so zealous in a right way, so devoted that the Lord says, "Although that whole area was going to go over to darkness, we will hold it back." It is like sometimes in the New Testament when people pleaded with the Lord and in the end He said, "Very well, I will do it." Our

Lord has not changed. There are times when He says, "I have not seen such faith for a long time as these people are exercising." On the highest level then it is a matter, not only of being built together as the house of God, but when we are built together, when there is some measure of relationship to one another, of then taking our position with the Head over all these matters.

I am not for one moment suggesting that we should politically try to determine things, or in one sense even economically, but I do believe we have a responsibility to see that darkness, the night, does not come one single minute before its time. We know the night will come when no man can work, but why should it come earlier? As far as I am concerned in this matter, I do not believe in those spiritual gloamings that they have up north. I believe in a tropical: day one minute and night the next, like a curtain that drops. Until that moment comes, we will stop it and that is our job. If you want to have a long, eerie sort of in-between, all right, but do not moan; you do not have to. You can keep those powers of darkness restrained where they belong until the moment comes when heaven says, "Now it is their hour."

Dear child of God, I believe all that has much to do with reigning. We learn lessons of being agreed in the Spirit, of being harmonized, of really having to get things right, of getting our corners knocked off that we never thought were there, and so much else.

On another level, perhaps more local, but very vital, no one will ever come to the throne who does not have a compassion for the unsaved. Do you think that God will one day put you in a position in His government when you have never shed a tear for another person? Do you think you can spend all your days without ever going out to witness or going to pray when there is an evangelistic gathering and still come to the throne? You will never come to it. Never. Not all of us can go out, but all of us have a place in this business of bringing others to Christ, and for some this is prayer. There are some people who think that as long as they have had a real experience of the Lord and know the deeper things, that is all that matters, even though they have a hard, cold, pious kind of facade.

Our Lord came to the throne because He was prepared to lay down His life for us. No one else will ever come to the throne unless they are prepared also to lay down their life for others. May God speak to us on this matter and may we see just how amazing it is that the Lord wants us to be with Him, set on high over the nations. That is what it says in those wonderful words in Deuteronomy 28:

> *The Lord thy God shall set thee on high above all the nations; you shall be the head and not the tail; you shall be above only and not beneath. You shall lend but not borrow.*

It means that the church will be able to do things for the locality it is in, for the nation in which it lives, that will be a tremendous boon and benefit to all. It will not be dependent on them, not borrowing from them, but lending to them. May the Lord make us such overcomers.

THE CONSTITUENTS OF VICTORY

Revelation 1:10-14,17,18;2:26-28;3:12,13,21,22; 21:1-7

Revelation 12:7-12—And there was war in heaven: Michael and his angels going forth to war with the dragon; and the dragon warred and his angels; and they prevailed not, neither was their place found any more in heaven. And the great dragon was cast down, the old serpent, he that is called the Devil and Satan, the deceiver of the whole world; he was cast down to the earth, and his angels were cast down with him. And I heard a great voice in heaven, saying, Now is come the salvation, and the power, and the kingdom of our God, and the authority of his Christ; for the accuser of our brethren is cast down, who accuseth them before our God day and night. And they overcame him because of the blood of the Lamb, and because of the word of their testimony; and they loved not their life even unto death. Therefore rejoice, O heavens, and ye that dwell in them. Woe for the earth and for the sea: because the devil is gone down unto you, having great wrath, knowing that he hath but a short time.

Now we come to the concluding words on kingship, or reigning with Christ, or overcoming. This is a theme we find in the Bible from Genesis to Revelation, and this is a matter of vital importance. We pointed out in our last study that our Lord Jesus walked in the midst of the seven churches, those churches selected to represent the whole church of God in time and on earth, speaking to each of them. It is a noteworthy fact that He ends the message He has for each church with the same burden: "To him that overcometh, to him will I grant. . . ." Our Lord could have said so many things to those churches. He could have expanded on various aspects of the truth. He could have spoken about their calling in one way or another; but, to every church without exception, the burden of His heart for the people of God comes out: "He that overcometh, to him will I grant...He that hath ears, let him hear what the Spirit is saying to the churches."

We spoke in that time of three spheres of overcoming. First of all, it is an individual matter. You cannot hide in the mass or in fellowship. That is one of the great dangers at the present time in the moving of the Holy Spirit. For the first time in many centuries, we begin to see the real need of fellowship, the real need of the body of Christ to function practically, the real need to be living members of Christ, living stones, built up together to be a spiritual house, a holy priesthood, offering up spiritual sacrifices to God. Now, the whole danger is that we make so much of the corporate that we forget the great need for everyone to have his own original experience. There will be no such thing as overcoming unless it begins with the individual. There is no such thing as secondhand overcoming.

Then, of course, the next sphere in which we have to overcome is the corporate. How can we possibly know anything about coming to the throne of God, anything about being a pillar in the house of our God, if we are not vitally related to the purpose of God in our day and generation? It is no good just being related to the purpose of God and what He did in the Reformation, or in the great evangelical awakening, or in the beginnings of the Brethren movement, or even what He did at the beginning of this century, in 1905-1906. Indeed, even when we think of our brother Watchman Nee in China, in 1926; or Honor Oak; or in India, we cannot just go back. We have to be related, not only to the purpose of God in general, but we have to be related to the actual aspect of the purpose of God relative to ourselves, to the age, to the generation in which we are living. Whatever it is that God is doing now, you and I have to commit ourselves to that by the Spirit. After all, this whole matter of reigning with Christ is not that we are going to be all dressed up in glory and pomp and splendor and sit on some kind of golden throne as a kind of exhibit or ornament. The whole idea of the throne is that we might be enabled to administer the government of God; that we may be able to supervise the fulfillment of the whole will of God for a new heaven and a new earth. If you and I have not learned what is the will of God for our own day and generation and become related to it, what hope is there?

The Sunday-go-to-meeting Christian, who is always on the periphery, the eternal spectator, dithers around like a moth attracted by the light and yet is never able to commit himself. He is never able to take responsibility, never able to shoulder the burden of the work, never able, as it were, to become just a member of the whole. Such cannot be overcomers. We can have the whole doctrine of the church, the whole doctrine of overcoming, the doctrine of the future and get things absolutely crystal clear, but when we are just butterflies, flitting in and out, taking what we want, getting a little bit of blessing here and there, we will never be an overcomer.

Then there is a third sphere of overcoming which is so often forgotten. When we are being built together as the house of God, we should learn to know how to rule for God, how to reign with Christ here and now. We need to learn how to govern a locality from the secret place, how to rule a nation from the secret place, how to rule nations from the secret place. God has not relegated it all to the future. This is our training school, the school of Christ. Every believer has to be in that school if he or she is going to come to the throne of Christ. We have to learn how to get on top.

Now, my dear friends, this is why the inexplicable things come. It is not to the people who have sinned, who have been difficult, who have been backbiters, who have been gossips and slanderers, who have been lethargic that these things come. So often the people who have been pioneering, who have been in the forefront, the vanguard are the ones that have inexplicable things come into their lives, things that cannot be explained. Then comes the whole point of training.

Jesus said, "In this world you will have tribulation, but be of good cheer, I have overcome the world." Did He do that just to dangle it in front of our noses, as if to say, "Well, you poor things, you are going to have a dreadful time, but be of good cheer, I have got through." That is what it would seem to appear, but is that what our Lord meant? He related the fact that He had overcome the world to our being in the world with much persecution.

What did the apostle say? "By much tribulation you shall enter the kingdom." But, you say, "Are we not born of God? If we are born of God, are we not in the kingdom?" He didn't mean our position in the kingdom. Through much tribulation we enter into the place where we are not underneath, but above; where we are not the tail but we are the head. We know what it is to reign with Christ. It is not just some beautiful doctrine. God allows the enemy to come into our circumstances, into our lives; situations come to us where the whole surroundings would scream at us that there is no God, that His Word is not true. Every circumstance would shout at us and then, and only then, do we know what it is to overcome by the Overcomer in us.

That's why as a company of the Lord's people, we sometimes face such heaviness. You feel tempted now and again to run away to some place where it is all joy and bliss, where you can sit there in a kind of atmosphere where everything is beautiful. We forget that the enemy does not bother about some things. He can afford to let some children of God have a lovely time because they mean so little. But once there is the possibility of people being built together and related to the purpose of God, then every weapon in the enemy's armory has to come out. He has to sit on top of those people, turn them inwards, get them fighting with one another, bring in misunderstanding, heaviness or whatever it is. Don't we find again and again that we have to rise up and when we do, it is glory? We can suffer for weeks and then someone in some prayer meeting says, "It is time we stood up and praised the Lord." And we do so. We often say the same old things: "Lord, You are on the throne." (How many times have we said it?) "Lord, Your truth is forever." Suddenly it is as if the power of the enemy is broken and everyone feels a release. You know at last the siege is broken. It is over and it comes because we have declared spiritual facts. When we have declared the spiritual facts as a company of the Lord's people, instead of being under, we find that we can rule.

You cannot rule from underneath. You are too busy feeling the pressure on top of you; too busy feeling that everything is sort of hemming you in. But when you break out by the grace of God into what you really are in Christ, you find that this situation and that situation can be touched in the name of the Lord.

THE HEART OF OVERCOMING

What is the heart of this whole matter of reigning with Christ? I believe the heart of the whole subject is found in Revelation 12:11: "They overcame him because of the blood of the Lamb, and because of the word of their testimony; and they loved not their life even unto death." There are many different ways of interpreting this chapter. Whether you think it is Israel that is the woman and Christ is the man child, or whether you feel it is the church which is the woman and the overcomers are the man child, whether you feel it is a particular set of events that is going to take place yet, or whether you believe it is expressing what has already happened, or whether you believe that it is principle in symbolic form that we have here, the constituents of victory remain the same. They are not constituents of victory for a certain class of person, but for the believer. However you look at it, in whatever age they live, the constituents are the same. They overcame Satan, the accuser of the brethren, that serpent, the deceiver of the whole world, because of the blood of the Lamb, because of the word of their testimony, and they loved not their lives unto death.

We are moving more and more into a time of shaking. It is a worldwide shaking. We know that in every single level there is going to come this shaking, not only things on the earth, but things in the heaven. We also know that when the enemy comes down, knowing his time is short, things will be infinitely more difficult than we have ever experienced before. They overcame by three things: the blood of the Lamb, the word of their testimony, and the laying down of their lives.

For whatsoever is begotten of God overcometh the world: and this is the victory that hath overcome the world, even our faith. And who is he that overcometh the world, but he that believeth that Jesus is the Son of God? (I John 5:4-5)

No child of God can ever overcome by the blood of the Lamb, except through faith. No child of God can overcome by the word of their testimony, except through faith. No child of God can ever lay down their lives, except by faith. Try it. Try feeling, try zeal, try devotion. You will find it will not work. It is only through faith. You will never overcome by the blood of the Lamb except as you have seen who is the Son of God; nor will you ever overcome by the word of your testimony, unless it is to do with the Son of God; nor can you ever lay down your life, except through the Son of God.

THE BLOOD OF THE LAMB

Let us consider the first of these three constituents of victory, the blood of the Lamb. People sometimes speak very unscripturally about the blood. They speak about putting the blood on the door or taking the blood for covering, and in one sense it is not wrong. But what do they mean? I hear people say, "We take the blood; we take the blood." What do they mean? The blood of the Lamb is another term for the finished work of Christ. It speaks of the death of Christ and His accomplished, completed work. How wonderful! They overcame Satan by the finished work of Christ—absolute, complete, sufficient. There is not a single thing that the holiest child of God can add to the finished work of Jesus Christ, not if you live to be as old as Methuselah and are so holy that when you are dead and someone throws someone else in beside you, your very bones would set them up again like Elisha's. It does not matter how holy you are, how much you know of the Lord, how far you have gone with God, you cannot add a single thing to the finished work of Christ.

The apostle Paul went like the Concorde in front of every other aircraft, streaking away ahead of everybody, but he did not add a single thing to the finished work of Christ. He could not. Stephen laid down his life as a young man, martyred for his faithfulness. He did not add a single thing to the finished work of Jesus Christ. No one can add anything to the work of Jesus. Isn't that wonderful? It is finished, completed, and it is a sufficient work. Within it is the power to convert a sinner into a saint, the power to conform the ugliest, most depraved sinner into the likeness of Christ. Victory can only come through the finished work of the Lord Jesus Christ. There is no other way. "The Son of God was manifested to destroy the works of the devil." You can agitate day and night in your own strength, hurl epithets at the powers of darkness, do a war dance for weeks on end, and it will not even cause hell to shiver once. But when you stand on the finished work of Jesus Christ, when you declare the power and sufficiency of the completed work of the Lamb, then it is as if the whole of hell is paralyzed, immobilized. In an instant of time the whole front line of hell is immobilized.

God forbid that I should say that anyone should not get to know the Lord, grow in the knowledge of Christ, or go on to full knowledge. We need more of the Lord, but if you think your knowledge of the Lord is going to bring you to the place where you overcome, I have a disappointment for you. It is not your full knowledge, or your greater knowledge, or your growing knowledge that is the basis for overcoming, but the blood of the Lamb. The more you know of the Lord, the more you need the finished work of Christ, lest you begin to lean on your own knowledge. That is why it says, "Knowledge puffeth up." It is very, very easy, even when you get to know the Lord more deeply, to begin to feel, "Well now, I know the Lord; I have some experience." The enemy can trip you up in an instant.

Sometimes we feel it is zeal that is needed, and we do need zeal. There is nothing so discouraging as to see a lot of sleepy people during a prayer meeting. There is nothing like zeal. I remember a particular group that I had some association with in the past where I used to feel that everyone prayed in a gloriously phlegmatic and detached manner. It did not matter what was the emergency, it was always in the same beautiful, measured tone which everyone prayed. But the Scripture says, "The effectual fervent prayer of a righteous man availeth much." I think there is something very wonderful about fervor in prayer. If nothing else, it wakens everybody else up. When you have that lovely, silvery tone just going on in measured beauty, you find yourself just going to sleep. But then someone starts from their heart fervently to take hold of the Lord, and it is as if the whole time wakes up. We do not say anything against zeal when people go out to others for Christ, when they are prepared to humble themselves and go out into the streets to contact people, when people are ready to go to the ends of the earth in the name of the Lord. We do not want to downgrade or devalue that; but, if we make our zeal the basis for overcoming, sooner or later the enemy will deal us a death blow. There will come a point where we shall be down.

I remember the wonderful story of Hudson Taylor, that great apostle of faith. He had seen triumph after triumph after triumph through faith and was always saying that God can if you have faith. But in inland China, there came a point where he lost his faith because of a whole number of personal circumstances and other problems in the work. This was not his faith in God, but his practical faith or his working faith. For months and months and months he was as down as any believer could be down. No one could get anywhere near him spiritually because he felt that everything depended on his faith and now he felt he had no faith; so obviously God could do nothing. Then one day he read that wonderful little word:

> *Faithful is the saying: For if we died with him, we shall also live with him: if we endure, we shall also reign with him: if we shall deny him, he also will deny us: if we are faithless, he abideth faithful. (II Timothy 2:11-13a)*

He could not believe it so he read it again: "If we are faithless. . ." It should have gone on, "He will desert us." But it said, "If we are faithless, He abideth faithful, for He cannot deny Himself." Suddenly he saw that it was not his faith that was the key to everything, but God's *faithfulness.* That is just putting it again in this way: "They overcame Satan by the blood of the Lamb."

It is not your zeal, it is not your works, but it is what HE has completed and finished. On the ground of that finished work there is not a single condemnation or accusation that can be leveled against you in either heaven or earth or in hell that God will accept. Now think about it!

> *Who shall lay anything to the charge of God's elect? It is God that justifieth; who is he that condemneth? It is Christ Jesus that died, yea rather, that was raised from the dead, who is at the right hand of God, who also maketh intercession for us. (Romans 8:33-34)*

There is only one way you and I can face the devil and that is with Christ as our righteousness. Now, do not think of this as kindergarten stuff. Amy Carmichael once said, "It seems a strange fact in Christian experience that some of the greatest saints, when they come to the last phase of their earthly life, go through a troubled patch of darkness."

We have many weaknesses in this whole matter of justification. Our preaching of the gospel has been so weak, such a decision-type preaching that many of us who have been truly saved do not realize exactly what it means to be justified. Therefore, the enemy knows there is a weakness, a terrible weakness, and sooner or later he can come with his accusations and condemnations. Now, he may condemn some of you and get you down in a way that would not do a thing to me. The way he can condemn and accuse me is not necessarily the way he would get you. Then again, it is amazing the things that get some people down. I have known people who have been in darkness for months. They have been unable to praise the Lord or enjoy the Lord or read the Word or feed upon the Word, and when finally they get the thing out which they feel to be so terrible, you just wonder, "What on earth is wrong with them. Are they mental?" But of course it is the accusing force of Satan. We do not know what it is to have the garment of salvation really upon us and know how to put it on. The enemy can get at us.

I remember an old sister who had such an influence on me in my younger days who lived just up the road here. I could never understand it when she used to tell me how she spent sleepless nights with the enemy condemning her and condemning her. As many of you know she was an opera singer. She married another opera singer, and they put their career first and their family second. When their first boy came along she asked a sister to look after him so that she and her husband could continue their work in the art world together. Of course they were not believers then, but later she came to the Lord. Her son rose to be head of the BBC Foreign Service, but there was a shadow between him and his mother. All through her life that thing used to keep her up night after night. She used to say to me, "I take the Lord as my righteousness and have times of worship."

I used to think, "Whatever is she talking about? Why does she worry so much about such a thing?" But if you do not know the accusing force of the enemy and do not know his power to come at you, you do not understand that the only way through is by the blood of the Lamb.

There is much more to say about this matter of the blood of the Lamb. You see, it does not matter what need you have, in the finished work of Jesus Christ that need has been met. It is not only justification, it is everything. Do you need to know something of practical holiness? Do you need to know what it is to be crucified with Christ and to live in the power of His resurrection? It is all in the finished work of Jesus Christ. Never think you can crucify yourself. People say, "I am trying to crucify myself." My word, they have a job. They seem to get the nail in one hand and when they are about to get the nail in the other, the first hand comes back off again. It is a terrible job trying to crucify yourself. People who spend their time trying to crucify themselves are so miserable. Have you noticed that? There is never a light in their eyes or a smile on their lips. They seem to have a suffering complex. They get to such a pitch that they cannot even enjoy a flower without feeling a twinge of conscience.

You will never know what it is to be crucified with Christ unless you see that first of all God has already done it. You are crucified because you *have been* crucified. Until God reveals that to you, you cannot live a crucified life. You cannot know what it is to live in the power of His resurrection until you see that the Spirit of God is within you. When you see the indwelling nature of the Spirit of God, then all kinds of things can happen in your life. You need to be conformed more to the image of God's Son, but if you try to do this yourself, you will have a hard job. The more you try to be like Him the more artificial you will become. When you see that it is Christ in you who is the hope of glory, that it is the work of the Holy Spirit to conform you to the image of God's Son, and it is foreordained as you cooperate and obey the law of the Spirit of life in Christ Jesus, then you are free from the law of sin and death and that work of conforming goes on.

Do you need to know the anointing of the Holy Spirit? Do you need to know the gifts, the equipment of the Holy Spirit? Some people get into such a tizzy on this thing. They feel like they have got to work themselves up into some kind of spiritual fury before it happens, as if by getting themselves into a spin they will finally take off. It is the finished work of the Lord Jesus Christ that has obtained the promise of the Spirit for you. It is on the basis of His finished work that Jesus, when He arose, ascended to the right hand of God the Father and received the promise of the Spirit and poured forth this which you see and hear. When we see that, we overcome. Can anyone overcome Satan except by the power of the Spirit?

> *Not by might, nor by power, but by my Spirit, saith the Lord of hosts. Who art thou, O great mountain? before Zerubbabel thou shalt become a plain; and he shall bring forth the top stone with shoutings of Grace, grace, unto it. (Zechariah 4:6-7)*

How can this work be completed? How can the mountain of problem and difficulty, of obstacle, become a plain, a highway for the Lord? It is only by the Spirit. Sometimes we are strangers to the work of the Holy Spirit, afraid to ask for more, afraid to seek for more, afraid to claim what is ours. But once we have seen the need, then we can get into error by thinking we have now got to provide a new basis upon which God will baptize us with the Spirit, empower us with the Spirit, anoint us with the Spirit. No, there is only one basis, and that is why some people who are older in the Lord just do not come in. They are looking for something, a basis that they can lay, and then they see someone who is quite an unsavory type find the Lord. He not only gets converted, but gets baptized with the Spirit as well and gifted. It makes you feel quite sick when you have been in the service of the Lord for some time. You feel there must be something counterfeit about it. "I have been on the road for twenty years and there is so and so; he has been saved for one and a half years, and a pretty unsavory character anyway, and he gets right in."

Do you remember that marvelous testimony of Alec Buchannan? Everyone in the whole house seemed to get an experience of the Holy Spirit except him, and in the end he was so upset with the Lord, he stormed up to his bed. He said, "Lord, I am sick to death of the whole thing. Here I am laboring for You for twenty years, and all these others I have lead to the Lord have entered in, but not me. I think the whole thing is bosh." That is exactly what he said. He got into bed and received a tremendous experience of the Lord. I cannot help feeling the Lord has a great sense of humor at times on these things.

The fact of the matter is that it is upon the basis of the finished work of Jesus Christ that God saves us, justifies us, sanctifies us, conforms us to the image of God's Son, brings us to the place where we know what it is to be crucified with Christ and to live in the power of His resurrection, anoints us with the Holy Spirit, and gifts us in the Holy Spirit. Everything we need for church life and the building up of the church is there, too. We do not have to find new things, new ways or methods. It is all there in the finished work of Christ once we know how to obey the Holy Spirit and to plumb the tremendous riches of Christ.

THE WORD OF THEIR TESTIMONY

Unfortunately, some of our new modern colloquial versions just put something about their witness to Christ which is a very sad way of putting it. What is their testimony? Their testimony is Christ. May I ask you what is your testimony? You might say, "Five years ago I heard the Word of Christ, something touched me and I surrendered to Him." What is that testimony? Forget the details; what is the testimony? The testimony is Christ. It does not matter whether it was in a hospital bed or in the street, in a church gathering or in a great Billy Graham rally. It does not matter where it was; you met Christ and Christ became your Savior. In that moment you had a testimony. "He is my Savior." You never had it before. You do not say, "The historic person of Jesus, who lived two thousand years ago has made a great impression on my life." No, your testimony is that you met the risen Christ, or more correctly, the risen Christ met you and now life just isn't the same. That is your testimony.

Now what is *the word of your testimony*? Surely it is the declaration of your testimony or the communication of your testimony. We have mentioned before about communicating. You will never overcome until you learn to communicate. We have to communicate. This does not mean a great spate of people just giving their testimonies to one another. It means that you declare Christ, Who is your testimony. It is a declaration of facts. For instance, if I say, "I hope He is my Savior," that is not a testimony. But if I say, "Oh, I thank the Father, the Lord Jesus is my Savior," that is a testimony. I have declared something. How do they overcome Satan? By the declaration of facts concerning the Lord Jesus. "Who is he that overcometh the world, but he that believeth that Jesus is the Son of God?" (I John 5:5).

There are times when you and I feel as dead as doornails, and the enemy sees to that. There can be all kinds of things, physical problems, upsetting your sleeping rhythm, other things, and the enemy is well able to do it. He says to some little minion demon, "Get along to such and such an address and wait for so and so to open one eye. As soon as they open their first eye, say to them, 'You are in for a terrible day!' When they open their second eye get them on the second line."

We feel dreadful sometimes and we cannot really explain it. We wonder whether we are even saved. Now that is just the time for the word of your testimony. I think it is so important.

The enemy will say to you, "Do not be a hypocrite; do not praise the Lord. There are enough hypocrites in the church already without another one. Be real. You are feeling awful."

"Yes," you think, "I am feeling awful."

"Well then, don't praise the Lord; it's not real."

So you say, "Of course, I don't want to be a hypocrite," and so you feel worse.

Reject and resist the devil so that he flees from you. Get on your knees or stand up and really say, "Lord, I feel awful today." Many of us are afraid to tell the Lord the truth, that we feel awful. Why don't we tell the Lord we feel awful? He knows it very well; why hide it?

Instead we say, "Lord, I feel so wonderful today," and immediately you feel hot smite you.

"You feel wonderful? You were just saying how awful you felt. You feel like dying and now you are telling the Lord you feel wonderful."

You see, that is the kind of Christian artificiality we all get into and that kills our spiritual life. It is much better to say to the Lord, "Lord, for some reason, either it is the enemy or I have eaten something late last night, but I feel bad this morning. I really feel gloomy, Lord, but here are some things I want to praise You for. First of all, You are on the throne. Thank You, dear Lord, whether I am down or up, You are still on the throne. You do not come off the throne because I am down."

We get the idea sometimes that if once we are down, the heavenly cabinet has a crisis and resigns *en masse*, as if the kingdom of heaven almost has a paralysis. But we can praise the Lord that Jesus is still on the throne and that He is our life and that the truth endures. There are a thousand things which are truth that have nothing to do with your feelings, and once you learn to declare them, you find suddenly, almost unwittingly, you come out into the sunshine. The enemy cannot bear the kind of worship that people give to God when they are feeling bad. It means more to the Lord than when they are feeling good. Therefore, once the enemy begins to find that every time he gets you down you start declaring facts, he will change his tactics. You will find that a whole lot of minor aches and pains and silly little circumstances disappear because he found that every time he did it, God got more glory. You will have plenty of real problems without the imposed ones of the enemy.

Many of us individually and in our life together as God's people have things imposed upon us which have nothing to do with factual circumstances. They only have to be resisted in the name of the Lord. Sometimes the best way is not even to look at them. Sometimes the enemy starts up something down here in the hope that like a whirlpool he will draw you in so that you go around and around until you become so giddy that you are sucked right into the vortex of the thing. Sometimes you need to just face it, but other times the best thing to do is just praise the Lord for what He is and you find that this thing the enemy was doing disappears.

Think of every single one who has died a martyr's death. Didn't they overcome by the word of their testimony? Didn't they declare that Jesus is Lord when they were dying, that He was their life? This essential declaration goes beyond prayer;

it goes beyond supplication; it goes beyond even desire. It is the declaration of spiritual facts concerning the Lord Jesus Christ. Moses endured as seeing Him who is invisible. Everyone else we find in the great list of hearers of the faith came through by the declaration of their testimony, the word of their testimony. With their lips, they declared the facts which were not apparent to the naked eye.

THEY LOVED NOT THEIR LIFE
EVEN UNTO DEATH

I think this is one of our great problems in this whole matter of overcoming. We may know something about the blood of the Lamb and we may know something about the word of our testimony, but where we get tripped up is on this third constituent: "and they loved not their lives even unto death." Of course, it is speaking of actual martyrs, but no one who loves his body will ever die a martyr's death. No one who loves their own life so much, their own possessions so much, will ever be a martyr. It is not just a question of a physical laying down of one's life in martyrdom, it is a spiritual character. Don't you think our great problem in this whole matter of overcoming is self-interest, self-centeredness, self-ambition and all the things that go with it?

The Lord Jesus said: "He that overcometh, to him will I grant to sit down with me in my throne even as I also overcame and sat down with my Father in his throne" (Revelation 3:21). How did He overcome? He overcame supremely, by laying down His life. At Bethlehem, he did not grasp a position of equality with God; He let it go. At Jordan, at the mount of transfiguration, when He could have stepped into glory but came back, in the garden of Gethsemane, on the cross, He let it go.

Our self-life is always Satanic ground. It is a hard lesson to learn and some only learn it at the very end of their physical life. That is why our Lord Jesus said:

Verily, verily, I say unto you, Except a grain of wheat fall into the earth and die, it abideth by itself alone; but if it die, it beareth much fruit. He that loveth his life

loseth it; and he that hateth his life in this world shall
keep it unto life eternal. (John 12:24-25)

Notice the words *keep it*. It is not that God said, "You
give up your self-life altogether; you never touch it; you subju-
gate it; you suppress it, and one day in the kingdom to come
you will get eternal life." No, what He says is that if you want
to find the release of your true self, you must let your self-life
go, and when you let your self-life go, when you lose your life,
you keep it unto life eternal. There is no truer word. People
who have lost their lives for His sake and the gospel's are
nearly always the freest of people. They are so natural, so
spontaneous. They are themselves, and yet the Lord is with
them. They have lost their lives and found them unto life
eternal. So it must be with you and me if we are going to really come through. There is no other way to victory. God will
never have anyone upon the throne of His Son who has come
there by assertiveness, by self-centeredness, by selfishness, by
self-seeking. No! There is no place in the throne of the Lamb
for anyone who is unlike the Lamb. The only way is to learn
how to let go of our lives. When we start on that path by the
grace of God, then we begin to find that the way up is the way
down; the way to fruit is the way of falling into the earth and
dying; the way of power is the way of brokenness; the way of
fulness is the way of emptiness; the way of resurrection life is
the way of dying with Jesus. There is no other way.

These three constituents of overcoming will remain the
same right through to the coming of the King. If you forget
what I say now, may God bring it back to you should you ever
have to be in the tribulation or at any other time. But it would
be far, far better to let God start to work out the constituents
of overcoming in us now than to await the emergency and
then suddenly to wake up to true values. May God help everyone of us. The Lord Jesus wants to bring us to the throne.

I come back to that wonderful word in the New English
Bible rendering in Luke, "And now I vest in you the kingship
which my Father vested in me." May the Lord bring us to
such a place, teaching us the lessons of overcoming, of true
kingship so that we are prepared for that which lies ahead.
There can be no other explanation for the ways of God with
His children.

I remember Mr. Sparks, when he was over eighty, saying to me one day in a conference, "Isn't it strange? I have been sixty-five years in Christ and I learned some lessons. When I thought I knew, I discovered later that I really did not, and now I feel at last that I begin to know just a little. Isn't it a strange thing, that just when we feel we might have something to give to the people of God the Lord takes us." That is so true. It can only be explained by the kingdom to come, that God is training us for His government. May the Lord have His way with everyone of us. Amen.